Parables to Live By

By

John George Samaan

Third Edition 20,000 in print

ISBN: 0-9703291-0-5

Printed in Canada by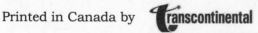

To Jesus of Nazareth

Contents

ACKNOWLEDGEMENTS

Most writers will agree that the greatest burden of sacrifice in writing a book is on the author's family. My daughter Rebecca patiently bore with me during the many weekends throughout the year when I wrote this book. I thank her for her love and encouragement.

I am grateful for Lynn Elizabeth Samaan for writing about her life's journey and her experiences with the poor in India. I am also thankful for the support and encouragement of my friends on the Board of Directors and the staff of the Boston Rescue Mission. I am especially grateful for Laurie Zimmerman for her help in editing and for Curtis Brettin and Eric Grenfell-Muir for their help in design and layout.

Numerous people read all or part of this

book and gave valuable suggestions. They include Herb and Beverly Moller, Dr. Elaine Phillips, Rev. Dean Borgman, Dr. Tony Campolo, Dr. Ronald J. Sider, Dr. Stephen A. Macchia, Rev. Roberto Colon, and Tom Harrison.

The work of the late Kenneth E. Bailey in his two books *Poet and Peasant* and *Through Peasants' Eyes* has been a great source of knowledge in my study of the parables. I am grateful for his years of experience in studying Middle Eastern traditions and for his insights into the parables of Jesus. His works were invaluable to me. I also gleaned insights from many other sources listed in the "Sources and Selected Bibliography" section.

The above is the known list of my supporters. There are several others whose scholarship, spirituality, and devotion to Jesus' teachings have had an impact on me through the years. Their ideas, sermons, teachings, thoughts, reflections, and experiences have sharpened my thinking while writing this book. After spending many years studying and reflecting on the parables, I am unable to trace these ideas and phrases to their specific sources, for they have merged with hundreds of others through the years. I'm grateful and indebted to all who have preceded me through the last two millennia for their reflection on these great parables.

PREFACE

How can a person who lived two thousand years ago change us today? How can Jesus' parables be a guide for our modern lives? How can these stories of the past become parables of the present? I hope that these parables, our own stories, and those of our friends will inspire you, guide you to a closer walk with God, and foster in you a greater love for all people—especially the poor, the suffering, and the persecuted, who are always close to God's heart.

I believe these parables have eternal meaning. They can help us understand ourselves and the world we live in. I also believe that Jesus' words can communicate to all cultures in all times.

In the first three Gospels, Matthew, Mark,

and Luke, 35 percent of Jesus' teaching was in the form of parables. In the Gospel of Luke, parables make up half of Jesus' teachings. Therefore, to understand the core of what he taught, it is important to understand Jesus' parables correctly.

Jesus' parables were spoken to Jewish peasants, fishermen, lawyers, and clergy approximately 2,000 years ago. Thus, the present-day reader may not always grasp their originally intended meaning. Accurate biblical meaning is that which Jesus intended to communicate to the specific audience that was addressed. Responsible biblical interpretation requires an understanding of the original context and of the historical, religious, and cultural perspectives of these parables.

I believe that Jesus' parables were not meant to be dissected and analyzed at the level of specific words or phrases. As a whole, they were meant to call forth a response and to impact the listener immediately with their point.

When Jesus was asked why he taught in parables, he explained that he was speaking of mysteries for his disciples and followers to understand, but for those without faith, the point of his stories was hidden (Luke 8:9-10, Matt. 13:10, Mark 4:10-12). On the other hand, many of his parables were for the people (Luke 15:3, 19:11), priests, and Pharisees (Matt. 21:45), or a lawyer (Luke 10:25-37). Sometimes, as in Luke 15, Jesus gave parables to disarm the critics that accused him of spending time with sinners. We can enhance our understanding by knowing to whom the particular parable was addressed and how those people would have heard it.

In many parables, Jesus used extended metaphors as a teaching tool. A metaphor associates two dissimilar concepts or ideas in a way that creates new similarities between them. To say that the Dominion of God is a man or woman sowing seed, making bread, or patching a garment is to create a new context for likeness between the realms of heaven and earth. As our minds open to new and complex associations, new truths may emerge from Jesus' teachings.

Parables serve to transform our understanding so we can reclaim the sacred story and spiritual reality. When we hear a parable, we need to catch its meaning involuntarily. It should affect us immediately and give us an experience or a glimpse of the realm of God. If we hear Jesus' parables as Good News for us, we already have a taste of what the realm of God is like.

Our Journey With God Toward the Poor

John's Journey:

Naeema's hands were rough and red from hand washing laundry—that of her family and her neighbors. This was how she made her living. Buckling under economic pressures and the mockery directed at two sons with Down's Syndrome, her husband had gone off to work one day and never returned.

The family had moved to the city from Upper Egypt a few years prior to our meeting. Naeema's two sons were teenagers, and her daughter was three years younger. The boys were both over six feet tall, which was unusual for Egyptians, and neither could speak. The striped pajamas they wore all day were generally soaked with urine.

Naeema and her children lived in the basement of a dilapidated tenement in Alexandria's ghetto. It was dark and stuffy, infested with roaches and rats, and filled with unwelcome odors. The apartment's floor was concrete and there was no running water. Sheets divided the room into bedroom areas; the bathroom consisted simply of a hole in the floor.

The first time I met Naeema's sons, I was 13 years old. I didn't know if I would be able to relate to them, but I kept on visiting them once a week. Before too long, however, I was walking down the road with one or the other of them hand in hand, a customary way of relating to same-sex friends in Egypt. I obtained for them the first job they'd ever had as helpers in the garden of my school.

One day Naeema appeared at my front door. Desperately, she pleaded for me to come with her and help her get her son out of the military. The oldest son had received a draft notice, and when he reported to the office,

the officials decided that he was not mentally challenged. They suspected, I suppose,
that he was simply playing dumb in order to
get an exemption. For 40 days he was kept
in boot camp. During that time, in attempts
to force him to talk, his superiors and peers
beat and mocked him repeatedly. Naeema
and her other children camped outside the
military camp gate during these weeks, beg-
ging for his release. When the military officials gave up and let him go, I hardly recog-
nized him; he was emaciated, exhausted,
and haggard.

A year later Naeema came to me again. A
well-to-do Egyptian working in an Arab
country wanted to marry her daughter and
take her with him overseas. Naeema was
elated. Yet I was suspicious and urged that
no plans be made until I had a chance to in-
vestigate the man. My inquiries revealed
that the man's real intent was to take the
girl to another country in order to make her
a prostitute—he had done so with other
young poor women. Thank God his scheme

did not succeed.

Through the years I have shared my life with people like Naeema who have modeled to me how to surrender and trust in God and the courage of sacrificing for the ones you love.

I was born and reared in Alexandria, the second largest city in Egypt. I grew up in a Christian family and always sensed a special calling by God. My mom had two heart-breaking miscarriages before conceiving me, and while experiencing difficulty with the pregnancy, she dedicated her child to God. Later in a dream, she felt the hand of God on her womb. She conveyed this to me years after I graduated from seminary.

As a Christian minority in a country with an overwhelmingly Islamic population, I experienced from early childhood the ugliness of discrimination. Ironically, these experiences strengthened my faith and helped to define my identity with God.

My father worked as an accountant for an oil company. As was true of most Egyptian industries after the 1952 Nasser Revolution, the government controlled this company. Our family struggled financially through most of my years as I grew up. Due to his Christian faith, my dad was constantly overlooked for promotion and salary increases. I recall the continual financial sacrifice my parents had to endure to provide for my younger brother and me. While the cost of living increased dramatically every year, my father's salary remained frozen. Every year we experienced more hardship than the year before.

My parents, however, were successful in enrolling my brother and me at Saint Marc College, the best private French school in the city. At school I was surrounded by Alexandria's wealthiest youth—some of whom had monthly allowances which exceeded our entire family's budget. Sometimes it was hard to fit in, but my brother and I excelled in our studies and in sports. In many ways, the school was an oasis for me. It was there at the age of twelve that I received the calling to know and serve the poor. I joined the Society of Saint Vincent De Paul, where I visited two impoverished families weekly in the ghettos. I served with the Society from the age of 12 until many years later when I immigrated to the United States at the age of 25.

After graduating from engineering school and completing my mandatory military service in Egypt, I met Lynn. She was leading a seminary team on a short-term mission trip. Lynn, a veteran missionary, had served among the poor in Calcutta with Mother Teresa. Our call to ministry among the poor helped us bond together.

I arrived in Boston on October 15, 1982, with a suitcase, a borrowed $200 in my pocket, and a faith amounting to half a mustard seed. The next few years were hard, challenging, exciting, and very formative.

While studying for a master's degree in business administration in Baltimore and a Master of Divinity in Los Angeles, I volunteered to serve among the poor. Later I worked as a Chaplain with the Union Rescue Mission in Los Angeles. A year later I became the Vice President of Services and Ministries. I helped the mission in its relocation and design of the largest comprehensive facility serving the homeless in Los Angeles.

In 1992, I was called to serve as the President of the Boston Rescue Mission. In the last 15 years, the mission has grown from a staff of two to a staff of over 30, including the support of thousands of volunteers. Today the mission provides a comprehensive continuum of care for its 35,000 annual guests and residents.

Throughout my past 40 years of ministry with the poor, I have met courageous men and women who struggle every day to survive the evils of poverty and destitution. They teach me about the priceless value and beauty found among the humble and poor in spirit. I find myself blessed by God's call in my life, for I continually see God's grace in the spirit of the men and women I serve.

Lynn's Journey:

Many of us who are working among the poor, the addicts, runaways, prostitutes, and others whom society classifies as marginalized people have risen from among those ranks.

My journey, however, was quite different. I grew up in a middle to upper middle class home in suburban America. The only remarks I recall hearing about the poor were either about the "changing neighborhoods" of the Bronx, New York, with its growing crime, (which negatively affected my father's business), disparaging remarks about welfare recipients, or an exhortation to eat all my dinner because of the starving children in Bangladesh. Sadly, we never sent food to those starving children nor did much to help the poor of New York City.

Then in 1968 I had a profound conversion experience accompanied by a call to full-time ministry. But even then I was a product of the Evangelical movement of the 1970s where evangelism, not social action, was stressed.

Nevertheless, I was eager to reach out and volunteered to help people in need: the mentally challenged, rural welfare families, nursing home residents, hospital patients, elderly shut-ins, homeless and addicts in the inner city missions, and at-risk kids. I even pursued a nursing degree in college to be able to help people with a practical skill, and I served for three months as a nurse in a bush hospital in Benin, Africa, upon graduation.

But even with all the good deeds of compassion, my heart was far from broken for the things that break the heart of God. I realized this painful truth one day in seminary in 1979. With only months to go before graduation, I still had no clearer direction for ministry than when I had enrolled three years earlier. "Why?" I pleaded with God. "Why won't you show me what you are specifically calling me to do?" The answer was not one that I expected.

I was led to take a course through Gordon-Conwell Theological Seminary in downtown Boston. This course dealt with the issues of poverty, racism, and even included an "urban plunge," where I lived and ate at shelters for three days and worked as a day-laborer in a factory. I was scared, humbled, and convicted, repenting for the first time ever for my hardened heart and sin against the poor. I began to feel the Lord soften my heart, but I knew there was still a long road ahead for me in this journey.

The next leg of the journey took me overseas once again—this time to Calcutta, India, to learn from Mother Teresa. She became my mentor and role model, and the poorest of the poor became my tutors. It was on Calcutta's streets and in her slums where I experienced a level of belonging, love, and healing which began to transform my heart and truly break it.

Unspeakable joy began to well up within me as I gave and received, learned and loved, and understood for the first time how unconditional love works. It was setting me free while I sought to give hope and a future to those lacking both. Over the years I have had the privilege to visit over 20 different countries and to share the love of God among the poor in many of these countries.

Then in 1998, I began to work at the Boston Rescue Mission as a chaplain. Unsure of myself at first, I feared the addicts would want nothing to do with one who was so unfamiliar with their world and struggles. But years of ministry had shown me that more than programs, wisdom, or help of any kind, people simply wanted first and foremost to be loved unconditionally and drawn closer to God.

Today that is what I love to do most. I listen to people. I love them where they're at. I pray with them, and I help them to experience the grace of our loving God. I help them to learn how to listen to the gentle voice of God speaking into their lives and helping them to feel arms of heavenly love that soak healing and forgiveness into the core of their being.

They, in turn, can reach others who are trapped in their own addictions, blinded by the world, bent over with guilt and shame and desperate to fill the God-shaped void in their lives which only God can fill. And in the process, love returns to me manifold. I learn from each one and am being transformed more like Jesus—who also called the poor his friends.

Lynn E. Samaan *is the Director of Spiritual Formation and Outreach at the Boston Rescue Mission. Lynn has traveled and ministered in over twenty different countries with ongoing projects in India where she leads teams every year.*

Lynn has a Bachelor of Science in Nursing from Columbia School of Nursing, a Master of Theology degree from Gordon-Conwell Theological Seminary, and a Master of Missiology degree from Fuller School of World Mission.

The Twelve Steps

1. We admitted we were powerless over alcohol — that our lives had become unmanageable.
2. We came to believe that a power greater than ourselves could restore us to sanity.
3. We made a decision to turn our will and our lives over to the care of God, as we understood God.
4. We made a searching and fearless moral inventory of ourselves.
5. We admitted to God, to ourselves, and another human being the exact nature of our wrongs.
6. We were entirely ready to have God remove these defects of character.
7. We humbly asked God to remove our shortcomings.
8. We made a list of all persons we had harmed and were willing to make amends to them all.
9. We made direct amends to such people wherever possible, except when to do so would injure them or others.
10. We continued to take a personal inventory and when we were wrong promptly admitted it.
11. We sought through prayer and meditation to improve our conscious contact with God, as we understood God, praying only for knowledge of God's will for us and the power to carry that out.
12. Having had a spiritual awakening as a result of these steps we tried to carry this message to other alcoholics and to practice these principles in all our affairs.

A Perspective on Homelessness and Addiction

Jesus' parables, his teachings, and his compassion guide us to a closer walk with God, and foster in us a greater love for all people—especially the poor, the suffering, and the persecuted, who are always close to God's heart.

Years ago, Jesus unveiled God's compassionate heart for my own life. I have spent the last 38 years ministering among the poor, homeless, and addicts. I have developed many close friendships among these groups of people and have had the joy of seeing thousands of lives transformed through many of the programs and services we developed to help them find their way out of despair toward a redeeming and fruitful life.

One cannot understand Jesus' parables without confronting those who make up society's disenfranchised. Let me share with you what I've learned about the complex issues of addiction and homelessness.

People often see homelessness and addiction as a condition caused by laziness, recklessness, or even conscious choice. Sometimes that is true. People make poor choices every day, and they often experience the consequences of those choices. But for the most part, an individual's descent into the world of homelessness and addiction begins very early in life. It may be caused by the death of a loved one, a family history of substance abuse or violence, abusive relationships, mental illness, lack of affordable housing, or inadequate public policies.

In fact, myriad situations can lead to homelessness and addictions of many kinds. Some come into homelessness by means of financial hardship, as the result of a change in a relationship, after struggling with mental illness, or through other circumstances one would never expect. It's worth noting that addiction is not limited to alcohol and the compulsive misuse of legal and illegal drugs. It also exists in more accepted venues, such as toxic faith and ideologies, sexual addictions, destructive and abusive relationships, compulsive gambling, the seductive lure of success, and the list can go on and on. At the Boston Rescue Mission, much of our work addresses the highly vulnerable population that is chronically homeless and their struggles with addiction to chemical substances.

Most of the people who become homeless and seek help at the Mission have already hit "rock bottom"—that moment when all the problems and stress in their lives overwhelm them completely. Their lives are in crisis and every crisis is interrelated. There's no food or housing because there's no money, there's no money because there's no job, there's no job because of poor health, poor health comes from the addiction, the addiction came about from poor choices, and the poor choices resulted from the pain of childhood abuse and neglect. It all becomes one big tangled mess, and it's difficult for most of these individuals to decide which problem to try to solve first. There's no time to stop and think.

For most people, homelessness is the result of deeply rooted personal difficulties. It is reinforced by failing public policies on housing, education, substance abuse, mental health, and inadequate discharge planning. The very term "homeless" can be a misnomer; the provision of housing alone neither cures a substance abuse addiction nor a mental illness. This misconception comes from the way some homeless advocates have defined and labeled homelessness since the 1980s. By calling the chronic addicts and the mentally ill who find themselves on our streets "homeless," it gives the impression that the common solution to their problems is simply to house them.

It is important to understand that a single-solution approach to solving the problem of homelessness will neither effectively recognize nor address the complex needs of this troubled population. The response to a person who is homeless and mentally ill should be different from that of someone who is addicted to an illegal substance. Immediate supportive permanent housing for a mentally ill homeless person may be an effective and adequate response, but it may not be the initial or the best response for a chronic addict. I believe that housing is necessary as long as it is supported by appropriate treatment and accountability. Long-term solutions to the problem require long-term commitment, an array of services, accountability, and genuine grace and compassion.

There are personal responsibilities to be expected from someone dealing with the problems of homelessness and addiction. It has been said that consequences and accountability are the addict's salvation! Addicts will continue to indulge as long as they feel that the rewards of using outweigh the pain. It is important that the addicts demonstrate a sincere desire for sobriety before enrolling in a program and that they will be held to that commitment or incur the consequences.

From my years of working and living among the addicts and the homeless, I have discovered that most of the issues faced by them come from a deeply rooted loneliness, rejection, brokenness, and lack of belonging. Most of them have been struggling with severe addictive bondage for many years. I recall the wise observation of the 19th century American slavery abolitionist William Lloyd Garrison: "Since the creation of the world there has been no tyrant like Intemperance (addiction), and no slaves so cruelly treated as his."

I also recall a conversation with a graduate from the Mission's recovery program as she described how the seduction of addiction made her feel "at home." She told me that when she was under the influence of drugs she felt that she belonged and her loneliness went away as long as she was high. But, as most addicts know well, these moments progressively worsen as the addictions take over the person and the loneliness and the void widen.

The majority of chronic addicts are unaffirmed people. Their core desperately needs healing through the gift of unconditional love. The greatest trap we may all face in our lives is self-rejection. When we come to believe the deceptive voices that call us worthless and unlovable, the destructive and addictive behaviors usually resurface. Self-rejection and societal rejection contradict the loving voice of God that calls us beloved children.

In my view, no services will bring a lasting cure to chronic human pain unless they address the issues of acceptance and belonging. Safe and affordable housing for our society's homeless is necessary, but I hope that we can envision the place called "home" as an oasis where we can belong. The power of a home is in its sense of community, connection, and how it helps us to see ourselves. It is a place of unlimited potential, an oasis where we allow ourselves to receive nourishment, light, and room to grow.

I hope the people we serve at the Mission discover their true selves and experience a supportive community while trusting that their experience of recovery will lead them to a place of true belonging in their own way and in their own time. The Mission can support them in that journey by providing them with accountability, support, encouragement, and resources.

Many of the men and women who come to the Mission daily have their lives laid bare; they are pushed to the brink of destruction by addiction, abuse, poverty, and destructive life choices. When they break loose from these bonds through their dependence on a loving God and the support of their peers, they become able to continue the long, humble road of healing. Their wounds are slowly transformed while becoming constant reminders of their need for God, friends, and continuing growth.

Bill Wilson, one of the founders of Alcoholics Anonymous (AA) describes his encounter of belonging with the loving God one night in his hospital bed. He was desperate after many years of the pain of alcoholism. One night, after Bill heard his friend Ebby's testimony about an encounter with God that led to sobriety, Bill W. cried out to a God he didn't believe in.

He describes what happened next:

> Suddenly my room blazed with an indescribable white light. I was seized with an ecstasy beyond description.....Then, seen in the mind's eye, there was a mountain. I stood upon its summit, where a great wind blew. A wind, not of air, but of spirit. In great, clean strength, it blew right

through me. Then came the blazing thought, You are a free man..... A great peace stole over... I became acutely conscious of a presence which seemed like a veritable sea of living spirit....

'This,' I thought, 'must be the great reality. The God of the preachers.' I seemed to be possessed by the absolute, and the curious conviction deepened that no matter how wrong things seemed to be, there could be no question of the ultimate rightness of God's universe. I knew that I was loved and could love in return. (Alexander 121)

Bill W. never took another drink, but the accounts of this conversion and his first drink are very similar. He even uses the same words to describe both experiences: "I felt that I belonged." I believe he began the recovery movement to share that sense of belonging with others and to help him sustain his own recovery. He described the journey of recovery from addiction as emerging from isolation to the knowledge of unconditional love. (Kutz 125)

Carl Jung wrote that alcoholism is a longing for spirit. The same word for spirit *(spiritus)* describes both the spiritual experience and also the poison of alcohol. Jung concluded that a spiritual connection could rescue one from alcoholism by giving an alcoholic the "spirit" he or she most longs for and needs in order to regain a sense of belonging. (Linn 64).

A relationship with God helps us to live with courage, to live transformed by love, which is what remains when fear is absent. God's hope for us is to live lives that are fully and fearlessly engaged, without hesitation, without regrets—belonging to each moment alongside God with the freedom and the courage to make these moments reach their zenith.

At the Mission we do not believe that we

have done our part by merely providing an emergency shelter bed and a hot meal, a job, or housing to someone who is addicted or homeless. In fact, this simply marks the beginning of a relationship of trust with our guests, where we can support them in their journey out of homelessness and onto the courageous journey of self-awareness, belonging, recovery, and transformation. Some of our guests call the Mission a "house of miracles," because they see miracles of transformation almost daily.

Although we celebrate many stories of transformation at the Mission, we also embrace our shortcomings because somehow, in the midst of it, the mystery of the communication of God's grace is present. Mother Teresa responded to those who pointed to her own failure to end poverty on the streets of Calcutta: "We are not called to be successful; we are called to be faithful." The mission is testament to that mystery of faith in both our successes and shortcomings.

When our guests enter the doors of the Mission they are invited to enter into community. The Mission tries to be a place of acceptance and love, but also a place of accountability and responsibility. Our vision is to become a healing community where lives are transformed through Christ's love, grace, and compassion. Community members are not expected to contribute money for the care they receive—even those guests who stay with us for well over a year as they pursue recovery, healing, and wholeness. They are provided with a bed, three meals a day, and daily support and treatment.

Community members are expected, however, to contribute what they can give to the benefit of the community. Perhaps someone is a craftsperson. He is given the opportunity to use his gifts to build shelving for fellow guests. Perhaps someone is a chef. She may be given the opportunity to help prepare and serve the 400 meals provided to the homeless on any given day of the week. Part of the healing process at the Mission is found in humble service to others. We are all in the same circle of healing and we have the responsibility to use our gifts to serve. Abraham Lincoln said, "Every man is my superior as he can teach me something." Everyone at the Boston Rescue Mission has something to contribute. Everyone is needed. Everyone has something to teach. Our graduates often show up at the weekly Alumni Group to share with others what they have learned—to offer support, encouragement, affirmation, and confrontation when it is needed. Alcoholics Anonymous recognizes this principle by simply saying: "The only way to keep it is to give it away."

Ironically, the accountability, healing, and care that is shared within a community such as the Boston Rescue Mission can reveal its own paths to healing in ways one might not expect. Some clients may choose to forego the opportunities to love others as they have been loved and resist the healing love of God. Such resistance often reveals itself through self-indulgence. Self-indulgence

contributes to chaos, disorder, and alien-
ation. Community is replaced with isolation
and isolation often leads to relapse and a
desperate sense of failure. The healing process has been detoured. But the "House of
Miracles" is also known as the "House of
Second Chances." Most of our graduates
have experienced one or multiple relapses at
one point or another while on the road to recovery. Even that desperate sense of failure
has been described by some as "the gift of
desperation". Many who experience a relapse
return with more appreciation and love for
the giver of life, with gratitude and a re-
newed zeal to embrace the recovery process.
They have been captured by the unconditional love of God and they have found their
way back home.

The greatest need of most people is not just
for food, clothing, and housing. Rather, it is
for unconditional love—to know that someone believes in them, that they belong in a
supportive community where they can contribute in a meaningful way and have a rela-

tionship with the God of forgiveness, who fills our hearts and always offers us a new beginning. Only love, acceptance, and true belonging can heal.

We must also address our larger corporate and societal responsibility to the social evils of today. We have within our power as a society to create policies that recognize the inherent dignity of humanity as a part of God's creation. This requires a conversion of heart focused on implementing change in the face of institutional evil. A fair society is not called to manage social wrong, but to bring adequate solutions to end it.

In the following vision given in the book of Isaiah 65:18-23, God lays out the following blueprint of the divine hope on how a fair society should manifest itself in treating its people.

> † *This society should be a delight and its people a joy.*
> † *The sound of weeping and of crying will be heard in it no more.*

† *Never again will there be in it infants who live but a few days, or elderly persons who do not live out their years; she who dies at a hundred will be thought a mere youth; he who fails to reach a hundred will be considered accursed.*

† *They will build houses and dwell in them; they will plant vineyards and eat their fruits.*

† *No longer will they build houses and others live in them, or plant and others eat. For as the days of a tree, so will be the days of my people; my chosen ones will long enjoy the works of their hands.*

† *They will not toil in vain or bear children doomed to misfortune; for they will be a people blessed by God, they and their descendants with them.*

God's hope is for all people to be given the opportunity for affordable and safe housing, adequate healthcare and nutrition, availability of good education, jobs and economic opportunities, fair laws and just leaders, and to have access to the knowledge of a loving God. A healing community should always be experienced in that kind of stability and hope.

To provide aid to people in distress is a virtue. But to ignore the cause of that distress is not. If we deliver services without challenging the systemic evil that is destroying the community, we are contributing to the dysfunction and eventually the destruction of that community. The task of a fair society is to continuously listen and learn from its vulnerable communities, and to hear the things that keep them awake at night and that make them weep.

The Serenity Prayer

God, grant me the serenity to accept
The things I can't change,
The courage to change the things I can,
And the wisdom to know the difference.

Living one day at a time,
Accepting hardship as a pathway to peace;
Taking as Jesus did,
This *broken* world as it is,
Not as I would have it;

Trusting that You will make all things right
If I surrender to Your will;
So that I may be reasonably happy in this life
And supremely happy
With You forever in the next.

Reinhold Niebur

Parables to Live By

Part One

Wealth and Wisdom

The Rich Man and Lazarus:
Living Righteously

Luke 16:19-31

"There was a rich man who was dressed in purple and fine linen and lived in luxury every day. At his gate was laid a beggar named Lazarus, covered with sores and longing to eat what fell from the rich man's table. Even the dogs came and licked his sores.
The time came when the beggar died and the angels carried him to Abraham's side. The rich man also died and was buried. In hell (Hades), where he was in torment, he looked up and saw Abraham far away, with Lazarus by his side. So he called to him, 'Father Abraham, have pity on me and send Lazarus to dip the tip of his finger in water and cool my tongue, because I am in agony in this fire.'

But Abraham replied, 'Son, remember that in your lifetime you received your good things, while Lazarus received bad things, but now he is comforted here and you are in agony. And besides all this, between us and you a great chasm has been fixed, so that those who want to go from here to you cannot, nor can anyone cross over from there to us.'

He answered, 'Then I beg you, father, send Lazarus to my father's house, for I have five brothers. Let him warn them, so that they will not also come to this place of torment.'

Abraham replied, 'They have Moses and the Prophets; let them listen to them.'

'No, father Abraham,' he said, 'but if someone from the dead goes to them, they will repent.'

He said to him, 'If they do not listen to Moses and the Prophets, they will not be convinced even if someone rises from the dead.'"

In the entire Bible I do not believe there is a story more stirring or more disturbing than that of the rich man and Lazarus. The parable is disturbing because of its portrayal of Lazarus suffering on earth and the rich man's suffering in the life after. It is the only passage in the entire Bible that describes the thoughts, emotions, and words of a person in eternal torment (Hades).

This is a story of surprising reversals. Although we are told the name of the poor man, the rich man's name is not revealed by Jesus. This is a reversal of how things in this world are done. The names of the rich are known, but the names of the poor are either not known, or simply not counted as worth noting.

Jesus described the rich man as dressed in purple and fine linens, which in Jesus' time indicated wealth. It is likely that the rich man spent his wealth on himself and that he lived in luxury every day. He was the type who today would wear the best designer clothes, drive a nice car, and enjoy life's pleasures.

This is the only parable in which Jesus gave a proper name to one of his characters. By naming the poor man Lazarus, meaning "God is my help," Jesus made us aware that the poor man trusted in God. He knew God. Not only was he poor physically, but he was also "poor in spirit." Lazarus' poverty must have worked to his spiritual good—lacking earthly comforts, he turned his heart to God and sought divine consolation.

Physical poverty, by itself, does not automatically produce humility, righteousness, or dependence upon God, though it can help. However, wealth is often a real deterrent to these three virtues. Of course, not all who are poor or rich will respond to God in the same way as Lazarus or the rich man.

It is important to note that Jesus did not portray the rich man as a cruel person. He did not say that he was an oppressor of the poor, a robber, a false accuser or an abuser of orphans and widows. In the parable, he was just a rich man who lived in comfort, while at his gate a poor man lived in misery. How long did Lazarus lie at the gate of the rich man? We cannot tell, but long enough for the rich man to know him by name.

What was the sin of the rich man? He had not ordered Lazarus to be removed from his gate. He had no objections to Lazarus eating the bread that was thrown from his table. The sin of the rich man was that he did not follow the instructions that God had given to Moses and the prophets by caring for the poor, such as Lazarus, in his presence. His sin was the sin of omission.

He simply accepted Lazarus as part of the landscape. He thought it natural that Lazarus should lie in pain and hunger. He never inconvenienced himself to help improve Lazarus' situation. It is what the rich man did not do that caused his eternal misery. The rich man missed the opportunities that

God placed at his doorstep.

One of the points we typically miss in this parable is that God may have placed Lazarus on the rich man's doorstep as much for the sake of the rich man as for the poor man. Lazarus knew God. If the rich man had reached out to him, Lazarus may have helped him to better know and trust God. We, as the wealthy and comfortable, need those who are poor as much as they need us, and sometimes even more. The poor are often models of compassion, generosity, and care for others.

I recall a discussion I had with a friend who came one evening to visit me at the Boston Rescue Mission. That night we had 200 homeless men and women spending the night with us. The smell can be strong and the sight disturbing. He told me that next time he would not be able to meet me inside the mission, as it was difficult for him to see the poor and to have a glimpse of their pain. Sometimes we, too, fall into the illusion that if we close our eyes, the suffering of others will not require a response from us. I believe that my friend missed a blessing God may have had for him that night. The poor often are the vehicles God uses to soften our hearts with compassion and open us to a greater faith.

Albert Schweitzer, a world-class theologian, surgeon, and one of the great classical organists of his time, was convicted one day while re-reading this parable. God began showing him that Africa was like Lazarus, Europe was like the rich man, and that he needed to do something about it. Soon after, Schweitzer left his life of ease in Europe to minister in Africa. God may show each of us a different way to respond to the needs in our midst. What is important is that we allow God to speak to our hearts.

The time came when the beggar died and the angels carried him to Abraham's side, a tremendous comfort and blessing to a Jew. The rich man also died and was buried. The day will come when we will all die.

Now the parable shows another reversal; Lazarus was comforted, while the rich man suffered torment. Lazarus, who lived in dependence upon God, was carried by the angels to Abraham's side while the rich man's spiritual poverty was intensified. He lived without dependence upon God in this world, so he died without God for eternity. Not only did he lose the finer things of life forever, but he also lost his opportunity to enjoy God—forever.

Now we have the rich man assessing his poverty and a poor man his blessings. The rich man, who did not see his need for Lazarus in his lifetime, realized his need for him in the afterlife.

Sweating in agony from the heat, the rich man looked across the great chasm and saw Lazarus in a state of bliss. He requested that Abraham send Lazarus to help him. He still did not get the message that he was doomed.

Abraham essentially explained the situation to the rich man this way: "Rich man, you have had your conveniences while you were living in luxury every day. Lazarus lived in the poor section of town. He grew up on a poor man's diet, he went to lousy schools, he could not find jobs, and when he got sick, nobody cared for him. When he slipped in the gutter, nobody noticed. But you grew up in the rich section of town. You had it all, but you spent your whole life digging a wide ditch between you and Lazarus instead of building a bridge. This ditch is the chasm that separates you from him now, and the bad news is that it is too late for him to help you. You are a dead man who missed his opportunity."

Does the rich man's fate mean there's no mercy or forgiveness for our sins? By no means. God had given the rich man clear instructions through the scriptures and a lifetime of opportunities in the person of

Lazarus for him to repent, to surrender his will to God, and to live righteously. But the rich man was so consumed with his self-centered life that he missed those opportunities. God does not interfere with our freedom to choose the way we want to live on earth, but instead gives us guideposts through the other people and the scriptures to lead us in our journey through life.

This parable makes it clear that God wants us to live in this world wisely, compassionately, responsibly, and charitably. Human suffering is a matter of eternal importance. God's concern for the well-being of people here on earth follows us to the grave and beyond.

The question asked continually by the Bible is, what is the focus of our lives? Do we live only for ourselves, our comfort, our security, our salvation, or also for others? Micah, the prophet, gave us his answer: "God has showed you, O man, what is good; and what does the Lord require of you but to do justice, and to love kindness, and to walk humbly with our God?" (Micah 6:8).

Jesus commanded us to feed the hungry, to shelter the homeless, to visit the prisoner, and to care for the poor (Matt. 25). To love God is to love people—not only our friends, but all people brought to our attention and across our path. That covers a lot of uncomfortable ground. Their welfare must be of a genuine concern to us because it is to God. We—you and I—form the primary representation of God's presence in this world.

The parable ends with a final twist. The rich man tells Abraham that the scriptures may not be enough warning to his brothers. He hopes for someone to come back from the dead to warn them. Surely then his brothers would listen and heed the scriptures. Abraham tells him if they will not obey the scriptures, they will not be convinced, even if someone rises from the dead. Jesus answered even this request; He returned from the dead so we might believe and obey.

A woman terminally ill in the hospital was weeping after being told she had cancer. When a friend sought to console her she replied, "I am not weeping because I am dying. I am weeping because I never lived." Her remorse came from missed opportunities to live and a failure to discover the unique miracle of her life.

If we do not find purpose in living, no one else can do it for us. The opportunities that life offers me, of course, are different from the ones it presents to you. Lazarus is not at my doorstep, nor is he probably waiting at yours, but someone is—someone physically or mentally challenged, someone who is abused, alone, or lost.

Lynn first met Sabina, a young Indian professional, during the summer of 1980 in Calcutta, India. Lynn was leading a team of students on a summer mission project, and both Sabina and the team were living at the

YWCA. Her job had relocated her to a city where she knew no one and permanent housing was hard to come by. She was lonely, and the team was eager to make Indian friends.

When Lynn and her team were not ministering among the poor of Mother Teresa's ministry, they spent time sharing with Sabina their faith and lives, while she shared with them her life and faith as a Hindu. Lynn saw her again the following summer, but soon lost touch.

In 1995, fifteen years later, Lynn had the opportunity to return to Calcutta. The city seemed darker, more polluted, and more crowded than ever. Every pastor or missionary she had known from previous trips had either died or had relocated. She oriented the team and planned to minister at Mother Teresa's Home of the Dying the following morning. She had barely arrived when she heard a voice calling her name from across the room, "Lynn!"

Who on earth knows me here, Lynn thought, as she turned to see who called. Sabina hurried across the floor, glowing, holding a box of sweets as she gave Lynn a hug. "What are you doing here?" Lynn asked, never having seen her serving among the poor before.

Sabina replied, "Shortly after you and your team left many years ago, I decided to come to the Home for the Dying and see what it was that attracted you to this work. I don't think I have missed a Saturday since, coming here bringing sweets to the patients and helping out. I've never known such joy, and you want to know something else? I'm now a Christian and regularly attend church. My life has completely changed direction since I first met you, and I'm so grateful."

I recall a conversation with a woman after I had shared that story. She told me that she would like to change but she did not believe that she could. Many of us have good intentions but are struggling with the fear of, or inability, to change the way we are accustomed to live. The Good News is that change is possible. It is never too late to change, especially when we ask God and then surrender to grace. Then all things are possible.

This parable is Good News because it alerts us to seize the opportunities God presents to us. Jesus is really saying; "Go beyond your comfort zone, to serve God now in the person of the poor, outcast, and broken of this world." He told this parable to challenge his listeners to act now, because tomorrow may not come. Jesus is inviting us to follow him. He already earned for us the costly victory of eternal life with God. May the Holy Spirit guide us as we seize our opportunities today and live lives which minister to God's people —the poor.

The Rich Fool: *Living a Life That Is Rich toward God*

Luke 12:13-21

Someone in the crowd said to Jesus, "Teacher, tell my brother to divide the inheritance with me." Jesus replied, "Man, who appointed me a judge or an arbiter between you?" Then he said to them, "Watch out! Be on your guard against all kinds of greed; a man's life does not consist in the abundance of his possessions." And he told them this parable: "The ground of a certain rich man produced a good crop. He thought to himself, 'what shall I do? I have no place to store my crops.'

Then he said, 'This is what I'll do. I will tear down my barns and build bigger ones, and there I will store all my grain and my goods. And I'll say to myself,

"You have plenty of good things laid up for many years. Take life easy; eat, drink and be merry."'

But God said to him, 'You fool! This very night your life will be demanded from you. Then who will get what you have prepared for yourself?'

This is how it will be with anyone who stores up things for himself but is not rich toward God."

In Jesus' time, people often called upon the rabbis to settle legal disputes. The law allowed the eldest son to receive double what any of the other sons received. The proportion of inheritance was thus fixed, and the plaintiff, in this case, had every legal right to receive his share of the inheritance. But Jesus answered, "Watch out! Be on your guard against all kinds of greed; a man's life does not consist in the abundance of his possessions." Jesus' words strike at the very heart of greed, the human desire for more and better. His teaching helps us to guard our hearts from wanting more. Jesus' followers needed to learn the lesson that joy, success, and fulfillment in life are not dependent upon material things. To make his point, Jesus told a parable about a rich man. This parable does not directly address the accumulation of wealth, but it does examine the problem of what the wealthy should do with their riches.

The main character of this parable is a wealthy landowner. Jesus portrays the landowner as one who plans for a long future, but fails to realize the true source of wealth and the righteous response that wealth demands. This rich landowner wants to build bigger and bigger barns to store surplus grain and goods. The assumption is that an easy life is ahead with provisions for all possible needs. God sees this as foolish because life can end suddenly and unexpectedly, and wealth helps nothing. It simply passes on to someone else. This landowner's sin was not gaining more income, but hoarding it and becoming a slave to it instead of sharing generously.

One of the more significant points in this parable is that the land produced such an abundant harvest that the existing storage facilities were incapable of holding all the crops. For a crop to be that abundant suggests a divine blessing. The attitude should have been, "How should I respond to this gracious blessing from God?" But, unfortunately, the landowner was neither grateful nor "rich toward God."

The landowner was self-focused. Instead of sharing the surplus with people in need, the landowner decided to tear down all of the existing barns in order to build bigger ones. Neither the poor, nor the welfare of the community, nor the work of God were considered. But God's plan for us may be very different from our own. God may decide that others should share the extra blessing of abundance. Once we are gone, our earthly riches cannot follow us.

Today in America, we are seeing a new love affair with huge houses. As the family size is shrinking, the size of new houses is increasing. These homes start at around 4,000 square feet. If you want to keep up with the current trend, a 2,500 square feet home will not do. Who is moving into these vast spaces? Surprisingly, "empty-nesters"—folks between the ages of 55 to 65—are the prime buyers.

We are consumed with consuming. We want to have the fastest, the costliest, the coolest and the newest. But the next time we reach for our credit cards or our checkbooks, we need to ask ourselves, "Where is my treasure?" Let us remember that most of the things we buy end up consuming our precious time and often possess us. Junkyards bring us an alarming message. They are full of possessions that people worked hard for and sacrificed to buy. Now those things are mere junk that is thrown away.

The richest people in this world are people who are rich toward God and follow the steps of Jesus in bringing hope to people's lives. The truly rich are found serving among the poor, blessing the sick in hospitals, befriending the lonely, hugging people with leprosy, sharing with others the blessings that God has given them. The God of the Bible is a compassionate God who provides richly. We have access to the source of the true treasures of life, God's grace and love. By God's grace and love we are all richly blessed.

When we experience the death of someone we love, it often helps us to put our lives into perspective. Confronting death opens our eyes to ordering our priorities and sorting out the things that are really important. We are able to see clearly what should be the focus of our lives, where we should put our attention and effort. Death helps us to answer the important question, "How can we be rich toward God—living life in such a way as to honor God, other people, and ourselves?"

How many of us have thought, "When we have the time, we will do more for God; spend more quality time with our family and friends; do more to help people in need; share the Good News with others; give more of our money, talents and time to make a difference in this world?"

But not now. The bills have to be paid, the house needs to be remodeled, more barns need to be built, and the list goes on and on. Have you noticed that often the most important things in life get neglected? We find it easy to postpone developing healthy relationships, reaching out to people in need, and being rich toward God.

For what do we want to be remembered? Jesus is reminding us that our lives are made for much more than building bigger barns. We may not have tomorrow. It is not guaranteed. We only have today.

I do not want to be remembered as a person who went to work on time, was good at his work, lived in a nice house, and drove a new car. Someday someone will stand at my funeral and will have to summarize my life in a few words. There is nothing wrong with the above list, but it is not how I want to be remembered. My life is a gift from God, a miracle. I was created to share that miracle by leaving the world a better place.

I've known Peter, a successful business executive, since the early nineties. He was Vice President of Finance for a Fortune 200 company for a number of years. He joined his firm in the mid-1960s, right out of graduate business school. Peter built a long and successful career, starting at corporate headquarters in Boston, then in Montreal, Frankfurt, and back again in Boston.

His work was demanding at times, but he relished the challenges and very much liked what he was doing. Still, he wasn't satisfied—something was missing. It dawned on

Peter that promotions, titles and stock options were not the way to discover meaning in life or achieve success.

Peter became a committed Christian while living in Germany as he neared fifty. The change came gradually. During this time, he witnessed the transformed life of his wife. Curious, he delved into the Bible, <u>Mere Christianity</u> by C.S. Lewis, and other spiritual books that now graced his wife Beverly's nightstand. His faith grew, especially through the study of the parables of Jesus. Something else grew with his faith, however: a desire to invest his time, resources, energy and talents in people in need. He wanted to live as Jesus would have him live.

"How much is enough?" Peter would often ask himself in the years after they had returned from abroad. He could go on earning a hefty salary with incentives—or he could opt for early retirement and apply the talents God gave him toward helping others. Finally, after discussing his conviction with Beverly, they concluded there was more than enough to cover their needs, so in 1997 Peter quit his job. But he didn't intend to take it easy. His desire was to discover "the good works God has prepared in advance" for him to do.

Peter served as an active participant on the boards of the Salvation Army and the Boston Rescue Mission. At the Mission, he helped to found On the Job, Inc., a non-profit company that trains people who become homeless and provides work, housing and health care benefits. He was an advocate for a refugee couple facing difficulties in America and now mentors a recovering drug addict. Currently, he applies his know-how to assist people with their indebtedness problems. He helps families leaving homeless shelters to start new lives by collecting donated furniture and physically moving the families into new homes. Peter leads the board of his church, teaches Sunday School, and drives poor children to worship and to Christian summer camps. Together with his wife, he established a private foundation that provides seed money for start-up programs for the poor around the world.

Peter now serves a different Master. His desire is to be "rich toward God" as Jesus taught, *"Sell your possessions and give to the poor. Provide purses for yourselves that will not wear out, a treasure in heaven that will not be exhausted, where no thief comes near and no moth destroys. For where your treasure is, there your heart will be also."*
Luke 12:33-34

The Shrewd Manager:
Living Wisely

Luke 16:1-13

Jesus told his disciples: "There was a rich man whose manager was accused of wasting his possessions. So he called him in and asked him, 'what is this I hear about you? Give an account of your management, because you cannot be manager any longer.' The manager said to himself, 'what shall I do now? My master is taking away my job. I'm not strong enough to dig, and I'm ashamed to beg—I know what I'll do so that, when I lose my job here, people will welcome me into their houses.'

"So he called in each one of his master's debtors. He asked the first, 'How much do you owe my master?' 'Eight hundred gallons of olive oil,' he replied. The man-

ager told him, 'Take your bill, sit down quickly, and make it four hundred.'

"Then he asked the second, 'and how much do you owe?' 'A thousand bushels of wheat,' he replied. He told him, 'Take your bill and make it eight hundred.' The master commended the dishonest manager because he had acted shrewdly. For the people of this world are shrewder in dealing with their own kind than are the people of the light. I tell you, use worldly wealth to gain friends for yourselves, so that when it is gone, you will be welcomed into eternal dwellings.

"Whoever can be trusted with very little can also be trusted with much, and whoever is dishonest with very little will also be dishonest with much. So if you have not been trustworthy in handling worldly wealth, who will trust you with true riches? And if you have not been trustworthy with someone else's property, who will give you property of your own?

"No servant can serve two masters. Either he will hate the one and love the other, or he will be devoted to the one and despise the other. You cannot serve both God and Money."

In this story a dishonest manager discovered that his boss had found out about his mismanagement. And so, the manager decided to risk everything on the mercy of the boss and the gratitude of friends. To fail would be to face time in jail; to succeed meant being spared an unpleasant fate. The manager took the risk and was praised for it. It is cleverness, not mismanagement, that earns commendation by the boss.

The setting of the parable is rural Israel, where a rich landowner had hired a manager (the steward) with authority to carry out the day-to-day business of the estate. The manager can make sales and loans, and collect, forgive, and pay off debts for the landowner.

The manager earns a living by making commissions from all the deals he enacts on behalf of the owner. Most likely, the debtors were either renters who had agreed to pay a fixed amount of produce for their annual rent or merchants who had purchased goods from the estate for which they had not yet paid. The manager was wasting the landowner's possessions and possibly making money under the table. The accounts were not accurately reflected in the books.

The landowner acted on the suspicion that the manager had wasted and embezzled money belonging to the estate. He was called to the landowner and dismissed from employment. The manager said nothing in defense; the charges were true. The landowner showed mercy by only firing the manager. He could have also sent the manager to jail.

To be human, according to the Bible's teaching in Genesis 2, is to be a steward. As in this parable, the manager oversees what belongs to the landowner. The Bible teaches us that the earth belongs to God. Human beings are God's caretakers. Stewardship extends to many areas: the care of relationships, the physical world we live in, the resources with which we've been entrusted, and the sanctity of life itself. The day will come when we will all be required to present our stewardship accounts to God. We will have to respond to how we cared for the environment, the poor, all our brothers and sisters, young and old, and for how we cared for our bodies, minds, souls, and the resources, opportunities, and talents we were given.

We live in a time where waste is the norm. We see abundance as a blessing from God. But unfortunately, we can mismanage this blessing and neglect the responsibility of our stewardship to God. Are we, like this steward, prepared to be charged with wasting what is God's?

At first, the panicked manager did not know

how to proceed. He contemplated his future. Who would hire him? He wasn't strong enough for manual labor and was too proud to beg. He needed to change his public image. And so, he planned to risk everything upon his understanding of the mercy he had already experienced from his boss and upon making new friends who would help him if his plan didn't work. If he succeeded, he would be a hero in the community.

Since the tenants did not know yet that he was fired, he acted fast. He called in the debtors one by one. He did not give a group discount, but made deals and did favors person by person. He made people feel special. He wanted them to know he was their advocate and friend. He showed kindness and mercy to each of them.

The manager sought to win friends by reducing the bills of their creditors. Most likely, he reduced the interest portion of the debts, a reduction that may have amounted to as much as 50 percent. Although the Mosaic Law forbade interest (except for loans to foreigners), there were loopholes often used by the landowners. The manager's action understandably made him popular. He hoped that in his own hour of need, the debtors would remember his kindness toward them.

The debtors had no clue that the manager was not empowered by the landowner to make the deals. If they had known, they would not have been in agreement, because they would be breaking the landowner's trust and might then no longer be welcome as tenants. The manager naturally took credit for having interceded on the debtors' behalf for the reduction of debts. The plan was a stroke of genius because it accomplished a three-fold goal: first, the landowner's lavish generosity was praised in the minds of the debtors; second, the debtors were pleased with the savings; and third, the manager strengthened the relationship with the community as its advocate and friend.

The manager delivered the newly changed accounts to the landowner. The landowner contemplated the options of how to deal with this situation. The debtors were surely celebrating the landowner's generosity, as word of mouth travels fast in a small village. The debtors would now praise a generous and noble landowner. There were two options. The debtors could hear the full story, but then the landowner's reputation may be hurt. The second option was simply to accept the situation.

The landowner reflected on the two options, and praised the manager for his cleverness. He understood that the manager took a great risk by depending on the landowner's merciful nature. The landowner absorbed the loss and paid the price for the manager's salvation. The landowner showed unusual mercy, the kind of grace that can look foolish to the world.

The manager is not a moral model for anyone. But to his credit, he used his wits to make friends and feather his own nest in such a way that he gained commendation from his boss. He also knew that he could depend upon the generosity and grace of his boss. If this dishonest man solved his problems by relying on the mercy of his boss, how much more grace will we receive when we trust in God's mercy and generosity?

It is not that Jesus wants us to copy the manager's morals, but rather, he highlights how the manager dealt with the crisis. He saw the necessity for bold action while there was time. The manager was smart, realistic, alert, and had insight into human nature. He made the most of every opportunity. In Matthew 10:16, Jesus suggests that being a little streetwise might be a good idea: "Be as shrewd as snakes and as innocent as doves." The children of this world are wiser than the children of light. Jesus is encouraging us to develop our ingenuity. Material possessions should be used to help others and to build relationships in our lifetime.

Jesus told a story about a man who was as flawed and human as anyone I know. But he was a man who was also clever and shrewd. In a moment of desperation, he finally discovered the value of compassionate relationships and that he could surrender his fate to the landowner's grace. The landowner in this parable is not perfect nor is he a portrayal of God, but simply a generous person. It is clear that if an imperfect landowner can be trusted to be gracious, how much more can we can trust God's generosity, grace, and forgiveness?

In case we miss the point, Luke reports what Jesus says: "No servant can serve two masters. You cannot serve God and mammon." Mammon means more than money; it is the essence of wealth. It is whatever shapes our dreams. It is the core of what we value. It is whatever we worship. It is the thing to which we entrust our salvation. In theological terms, a god must be chosen and served. Saying yes to God means saying no to other gods.

Mammon can be many different things for us: money, drugs, sex, power, passions or self-fulfillment. In short, it is whatever we give our heart to and make as the core of our existence. The problem is that in giving ourselves to mammon, we end up still empty inside, unfulfilled and missing the intimacy that our creator desires with us.

Eight years ago, I met Dennis, a broken Irish-American man. Dennis was in his late 30s, sick with AIDS, drunk and high on drugs, and living on the streets not far from the Boston Rescue Mission. He was both liked and feared by most people who were homeless. In time I learned his story.

Dennis's parents were both addicts, and so life from the beginning was hard for him. Sadly, things quickly got worse when he and a number of older brothers and sisters were split up and sent to foster homes. In the foster homes he was sexually and emotionally abused. For Dennis, the world was not a safe place, and he began to think something must be wrong with him. The pain of abandonment stung, so he set up walls to keep from being hurt by avoiding close relationships with anyone. For various reasons, he was shifted from foster home to foster home. Dennis was robbed of the feeling that he belonged, was loved, or had anything to live for, and so he self-medicated with drugs and alcohol.

In his early 20s he met his wife and had his own two children. His first taste of belonging and family only lasted a short time. The nightmare-cycle began again as he watched his wife die in his arms from an overdose and stood helplessly by as his children were taken from him and placed into foster care. While looking for a place to belong he joined a gang, but soon found himself busted by the police and serving time in prison on several occasions. Over and over he tried detoxification programs but nothing lasted. It was just a matter of time before he was using drugs and living out on the streets again—angry, empty inside, and isolated.

"I've done so many awful things. I have never told a soul most of it. There's so much anger and hurt inside," Dennis once confessed. But after 14 years on the streets, Dennis connected with God at the Boston Rescue Mission. For the first time in his life he discovered that God loves him just as he is and offered him forgiveness and release from his guilt and shame. Dennis felt free. He was loved, and he thrived as part of the family at the mission. He quickly became a friend to others who were down and out— sharing with them God's power to change lives.

Dennis found peace and purpose in God while being a blessing to the mission— cooking, driving the van, helping at the reception desk, and serving the guests who came into the overnight shelter. Dennis's walls began to come down, and his heart began to grow. He still struggles with anger at times but focuses on the peace he has found, and he is finding his healing in Christ. On December 2, 2000, he married

Eva, his sweetheart of 14 years, and moved into his own home.

Dennis was in some ways like the manager in this parable: using and abusing the resources entrusted to him, dealing illegally, buying friends, and looking for acceptance in the wrong places. He finally met a merciful and forgiving God. He is now street-wise and shrewd for God.

Parables to Live By

Part Two

Compassion, Humility, and Prayer

The Good Samaritan:
Living the Compassionate Life

Luke 10:25-37

On one occasion an expert in the law stood up to test Jesus. "Teacher," he asked, "what must I do to inherit eternal life?" "What is written in the Law?" he (Jesus) replied. "How do you read it?"

The Lawyer answered: "'Love the Lord your God with all your heart and with all your soul and with all your strength and with all your mind'; and 'Love your neighbor as yourself.'" "You have answered correctly," Jesus replied. "Do this and you will live."

But he wanted to justify himself, so he asked Jesus, "And who is my neighbor?"

In reply Jesus said: "A man was going down from Jerusalem to Jericho, when he fell into the hands of robbers. They stripped him of his clothes, beat him and went away, leaving him half-dead. A priest happened to be going down the same road, and when he saw the man, he passed by on the other side.

So too, a Levite, when he came to the place and saw him, passed by on the other side. But a Samaritan, as he traveled, came where the man was; and when he saw him, he took pity on him. He went to him and bandaged his wounds, pouring on oil and wine. Then he put the man on his own donkey, took him to an inn and took care of him. The next day he took out two silver coins and gave them to the innkeeper. 'Look after him,' he said, 'and when I return, I will reimburse you for any extra expense you may have. Which of these three do you think was a neighbor to the man who fell into the hands of robbers?" The expert in the law replied, "The one who had mercy on him." Jesus told him, "Go and do likewise."

A lawyer asked Jesus about how to inherit eternal life. It is clear that Jesus was being tested by someone well versed in the Mosaic Law. He answered the lawyer's questions with a question of his own, and the lawyer responded by demonstrating expertise in the Mosaic Law. Quoting from Deuteronomy 6:5 and Leviticus 19:18: *"Love the Lord your God with all your heart and with all your soul and with all your strength and with all your mind"* and *"Love your neighbor as yourself,"* the lawyer articulated the two commandments by which Jewish scholarship and tradition had summed up the 613 points of the Mosaic Law.

Jesus then responded directly to the lawyer's first question about what he must do. The lawyer, wishing for loopholes, pushed the discussion further, desiring to justify himself; he asked for a definition of "neighbor," and this provided the opportunity for the parable. The lawyer was, of course, inquiring about whom he was required to love. Leviticus 19:17-18 identifies one's neighbors as one's brothers, "the sons of your own people." The lawyer understood this to include all Jews, but his loophole backfired instead.

The question was asked with the expectation that Jesus would answer, "Your relatives and your friends." The lawyer would then respond, "I have fully loved these," and Jesus would praise him for his obedience to the law. The lawyer was not really seeking information; he only wanted to justify himself. To his surprise, Jesus turned the question on its head. The parable not only answered the question of "who is my neighbor" but also, "how should I love my neighbor?"

All the images and characters Jesus used in his story of the unfortunate traveler were familiar to the listeners. The 17-mile, descending road through the desert from Jerusalem to Jericho has been dangerous all throughout history. It was a known haven for highway robbers. Bands of outlaws took advantage of the steep, rugged terrain. The constant trickle of travelers enabled some to make a career out of robbing those journeying back and forth.

The story intentionally left the man anonymous, yet a Jewish audience would naturally assume that the traveler was a Jew. He was beaten, stripped, and left "half dead." Then Jesus brought to the story a priest and a Levite, persons representative of the most law-abiding, religious, and learned citizens of the day. Jesus clearly used characters people would immediately identify as righteous in order to demonstrate how much more is required than mere observance of and obedience to the law.

The priest was probably riding a donkey, since priests were among the upper classes of their society. He faced a dilemma. How could he be sure the wounded man was a Jewish neighbor? When confronted with an unconscious, naked body, the priest was paralyzed. Not only was there the possibility that the wounded man was not a Jew, but he might even be dead. In either case, contact with him would defile the priest. Priests especially were supposed to avoid impurity from a corpse; Pharisees also believed they would become defiled if even their shadow touched the corpse.

According to the Jewish law, a priest should not touch a corpse, except that of a family member, or he would become ritually unclean for seven days (Leviticus 21:1-2; Ezekiel 44:25-27). Priests collected, distributed, and ate food tithed to the temple, besides performing other religious duties, and therefore took ceremonial purity seriously. If the priest defiled himself he could do none of these things for seven days, and his family and servants would suffer the consequences with him. The process of restoring ritual purity was time-consuming and costly. If the man was dead, the priest could not even approach God or his family before he was declared clean by another priest. Clearly the priest was a victim of the theological system. This situation was too complicated and costly for him. The task was better left to someone else. (Bailey 45)

A Levite followed the priest. He knew there was a priest ahead of him. On this road to Jericho, travelers were aware of who else was on the road because their lives depended on it. Muggers were common threats to all travelers.

The Levite, a man from the tribe of Levi (Genesis 29:34), who by his birthright could enter the inner rooms of the temple, is not bound by as many regulations as the priest. Both priests and Levites were actually from the tribe of Levi, but the priests were direct descendants of Aaron, the first of the priests. The Levites assisted the priests in preparing the sacrifices. They were only required to observe ritual cleanliness in the course of their religious activities. But, like the priest, this Levite investigated the situation, decided against offering aid to the dying man, and passed on. Fear of defilement may not have been his strongest motive. Fear of the robbers might have been. He might have said to himself, "If the higher ranking priest did nothing, why should I trouble myself?" In any case, he moved on.

While Jesus' disciples and some of the audience might have gotten a kick out of using two members of the religious establishment as the bad guys, they would have expected the appearance of a Jewish layperson next. They must have been shocked when Jesus introduced a Samaritan as the hero in this parable. The Samaritans were considered heretics and more despised than unbelievers. The centuries of animosity between the Jews and the Samaritans are reflected in the wisdom of Ben Sirach: "There are two nations my soul detests, the third is not a nation at all: the inhabitants of Mount Seir (the Edomites), and the Philistines, and the stupid people living at Shechem (the Samaritans)." (Bailey 48)

The Mishna (the Jewish oral tradition) declares, "He that eats the bread of the Samaritans is like to one that eats the flesh of swine." The Samaritans were publicly cursed in the Synagogues and a petition was daily offered up asking God not to grant the Samaritans eternal life. (Bailey 48)

Samaritans were the peasants of Israel's northern tribes left after all the tribal leaders were exiled, when Israel fell to Assyria in 722 B.C. When pagans from surrounding tribes were resettled in this region by the King of Assyria, these remaining Israelite peasants eventually intermarried with them. Samaritans were thus viewed as a mixed and ungodly race. They mixed their pagan worship with Jewish worship. Their only scriptures were a particular redaction of the five books of Moses, the "Samaritans Pentateuch," and they even had their own temple mount, Mt. Gerezim, as a rival to Mt. Zion. The Samaritans were not regarded as full members of the house of Israel. At the time of Jesus, the bitterness between Jews and

Samaritans intensified after the Samaritans had defiled the temple during a Passover just a few years earlier by scattering human bones in the temple court. (Heineman 48)

Jesus could have told a story about a noble Jew helping a hated Samaritan. Such a story may have been less shocking emotionally to the audience. Only one who has lived as part of a community with a hated traditional enemy can appreciate Jesus' courage in giving the story this twist.

Jesus continued. The Samaritan came close to the wounded man and took pity on him. He took the risk despite knowing that he could be a target of the same robbers who might respect a priest or a Levite but would have no hesitation in attacking a hated Samaritan. The wounded man was probably a Jew and the Samaritan could risk retaliation from the family and friends of the very Jew he was aiding. In spite of all these considerations, he was moved to help the dying man.

The Samaritan first cleaned and softened the wounds with oil, disinfected them with wine, and finally bound them up. He then placed the wounded man on his donkey and led the donkey to the inn. The social distinctions between being a rider or merely leading the animal are significant in Middle Eastern society.

His willingness to go to the inn and remain there overnight caring for the wounded man was not only compassionate but also courageous. Inns were not usually located in the desert; he most likely took the wounded man downhill to Jericho.

An American cultural equivalent would be an African American in the late 1800s walking into a Southern hotel with a raped and beaten white woman, and checking in with her to care for her wounds. His act of kindness would probably have been misunderstood and generated great suspicion. In the same way, if an act of kindness were to be done, it would have been more likely, and certainly safer, for the Samaritan to have left the wounded man in town at night when nobody would see him.

The wounded man, having been robbed, would have no money to pay the Jewish innkeeper. Therefore, if the Samaritan did not leave a deposit and promise to pay the balance of the bill upon his return, the wounded man, upon recovery, would not have been able to leave. The amount given by the Samaritan to the innkeeper is the equivalent of two days' wages. Depending on the quality and price of lodging, two denarii would be sufficient for a stay in an inn for several days.

Through this parable, we see Jesus reshaping the lawyer's questions. The lawyer wanted to know who his neighbor was and perhaps how many people he had to love to achieve righteousness and inherit eternal life. Jesus asked him, "Which of these three men do you think was a good neighbor to the man who fell into the hands of robbers?"

The expert in the law replied, "The one who had mercy on him." Jesus told him, "Go and do likewise." Jesus is saying: your neighbor is anyone in need; one cannot limit one's definition of who one's neighbor is, and one should strive to be a good neighbor.

The lawyer and the listeners found themselves confronted with a message of unconditional love for others. Unless we show love to all humanity, we will fall short of fulfilling God's commandment. The mandate is, we must become a neighbor to anyone in need. We must share God's love with all people, including our enemies. To fail to do so is to sin against God. The parable holds up an ethical standard for which to strive, even though we cannot fully achieve it. Like the command to "be perfect," it remains a standard to strive after even though, in its fullest expression, it is an ideal. But who of us is able to love unconditionally all the time? Who can meet that standard?

We can almost hear the crowds saying under

their breath (as they do in Luke 18:26), "Who then can be saved? What can I do to inherit the Realm of God? How can I fulfill the law?" The answer is, we cannot justify ourselves even if we do our best—the standard is too high. We need to surrender to God's grace to justify us. Eternal life is a gift given to us by the grace of a loving God. Jesus calls us to surrender to God's grace. When we entrust our lives to the Living God, we can achieve the impossible.

The year was 1995 on New Years Day. Lynn had been invited to bring her team of Americans to a special communion service at a leprosy colony outside of Madras, India. Never did she realize this service would have an impact on her life for years to come. She later recorded the story:

"As our van drew to a halt inside the gate of the leper colony, our team of twelve was greeted like long-lost relatives. After a brief tour of the colony, we were seated on metal folding chairs lined up behind a makeshift altar under a colorful cloth canopy. This tract of land provided by the government for the people with leprosy was about as undesirable as one could imagine. The surrounding hills were barren and the highway belched toxic fumes and constant noise. The lack of vegetation made everything seem brown and bleak.

"I scanned the poverty of this tiny community, which teemed with barefoot children. A few goats and mud paths threaded around a handful of one-room mud and thatch huts. Trying not to look conspicuous, I looked closely at the hands and feet of our hosts and tried to determine if they had "the disease." They seemed normal. A few stubs of hands and feet in the crowd and the telltale collapsed cartilage of the nose assured me we were in the right place.

"The communion service began without delay, as the bishop and pastors took their places next to our team on the folding chairs, and the people with leprosy took their places on the dirt floor. As I smiled at the bright faces of women and their squirming children, I did not realize that a large basket had been brought out, and hand sewn flower garlands were being placed around the neck of each pastor and team member. The air quickly captured the fragrance of their perfume. Fondling the soft petals in my fingers, I watched as a second large basket was pulled from behind the table and wrapped gifts were distributed.

"As I awkwardly waited my turn, I looked again at the poverty of the people and wondered why they displayed such generosity toward some wealthy Americans they had never met before. I received my gift graciously but struggled within, wondering if gift giving at a communion service was cultural. Then a third basket was brought out and from it came yet another wrapped gift. Now I was about to become emotional. Garlands were one thing, one gift was another, but now my sense of embarrassment and shame came full blown as I pondered the fact that I had come empty-handed; I who had so much, materially.

"The service continued. An upbeat chorus was sung to the accompaniment of a hand drum, and the bishop, who I could see was dearly loved by the people, gave a warm interactive sermon. One team member quietly slid onto the ground among the people. I wondered if I should follow suit, but a greater question was nagging me. How can I give something in return to these people? In my heart I began to pray, 'God, please, would you grant me the grace to minister your healing power to these dear people? May I be an extension of your hand?'

"I prayed earnestly over and over until I saw my opportunity. I filed in behind the bishop as he distributed the communion wafers down the rows of people. I quietly stood to my feet, hoping I was not making a major cultural blunder by laying my hands on each head. I began by praying prayers of blessing and healing. To my relief, the bishop encouraged other team members to do the same. Three others joined me.

"Soon the service was concluding with another chorus, but I could see something was beginning to happen among the people for whom we were praying. They were becoming excited. I could see it in their expectant, pleading eyes and by their voices, though I couldn't understand the language. I could feel the atmosphere of the place begin to change. More lepers lined up, kneeling at our feet, grabbing for our hands and placing them on their own heads, hoping for their miracle. Soon my hands felt as if they were burning with the power of God. With faith and expectancy I commanded sightless eyes to be opened. I spoke cleansing to the leprosy. We prayed and prayed, but nothing seemed to happen. Why wasn't God answering, when the Holy Spirit felt present and faith was so strong?

"Determined to understand the situation, I quietly left my prayer post to the others and approached the bishop. 'Why aren't the people being healed?' I asked in a straightforward manner. 'Lynn,' the bishop said with compassion, 'you don't understand, do you?' I shook my head. 'This is a service they will never forget for as long as they live. You see, no visitor who has come to these services before has ever dared to touch them. But you have not only touched them, you have held them, loved them, and prayed for them. God has poured out the Holy Spirit here today in a baptism of love.'

"Then the bishop asked, 'You see that man over there? He is a Hindu religious leader who has been a major opponent of this little church for years. He has never approached one of our services before. But tonight he was drawn by the commotion and stood watching for the longest time. A few minutes ago he approached one of the pastors who has just led him to the Lord. God is doing miracles here tonight.' I returned to my prayer post encouraged, eager to be a vessel of God's outpouring of love. I held these children of God close and prayed prayers, anointing them with the love of God.

"That night, back in our hostel, we debriefed, trying to make sense out of all that had happened. We still wondered why God hadn't healed. If anyone deserved healing, it was these dear people who had been dealt a horrid lot in life. We talked about how bad we felt that we'd gone empty-handed discussed our fears beforehand. Then someone suggested, 'Suppose tonight was not about the cleansing of the lepers but about the cleansing of our own leprosy?'

"The thought struck me. We had held back when we arrived at the colony, but they embraced us with unconditional love. We, in our wealth, had come with nothing. They in their poverty gave everything. We, who claimed to be whole, were really the ones with the leprosy—a spiritual leprosy that affected our hearts—making them numb to the heart of God. Indeed, my own leprosy was already spreading, causing its telltale symptoms of blindness and isolation. I was the one who needed to be prayed for by them. I now wished we could return to give them humbly the dignity they deserved as God's beloved children and to ask them to minister to us. I understood in a flash something someone had said to me years earlier, 'We need the poor more than they need us.'

"The summer of 1996 I returned to the same community of believers for a dedication service of their church cornerstone. It bore my name. I wept. This time I came with gifts and had the privilege of being prayed for—an experience I will never forget. As I knelt in the dust with my face to the ground, a gray-haired woman well into the advanced stages of leprosy placed her stubs upon my head; she spoke for close to five minutes in her native Tamil tongue in what felt like a prayer of healing and commission.

"On several subsequent occasions I have had the chance to visit this colony. I did not recognize the place; cinder block homes have replaced the mud huts. A community center has been built, and the residents are now busy and productive pursuing various cottage industries. The church is finished and now serves a neighboring community as well. I have had the honor of sharing in the baptism of radiant new converts from this colony who are experiencing the miracle of the new birth.

"Plans are in the works for re-vegetation of the area and better sewerage. The body of Christ there is still reaching out in love and healing to others who visit—others, like us, with spiritual leprosy."

The Pharisee and the Tax Collector: *Living Humbly*

Luke 18:9-14

To some who were confident of their own righteousness and looked down on everybody else, Jesus told this parable: "Two men went up to the temple to pray, one a Pharisee and the other a tax collector. The Pharisee stood up and prayed about himself: 'God, I thank you that I am not like other men—robbers, evildoers, adulterers or even like this tax collector. I fast twice a week and give a tenth of all I get.' "But the tax collector stood at a distance. He would not even look up to heaven, but beat his breast and said, 'God, have mercy on me, a sinner.' "I tell you that this man, rather than the other, went home justified before God. For everyone who exalts himself will be humbled, and he who humbles himself will be exalted."

Jesus saw that some of the people who gathered around him were prideful and judgmental of others. They relied on their own righteousness for their salvation rather than on the grace and mercy of God. Most likely, Jesus was in or near the temple at the time, watching the people who came to pray. Jesus told this story in response to people who looked down on others.

Two men went up to the temple to pray, but only one really prayed. The first was a good man, a pillar of his community and a keeper of the religious rules. He was so good that he could hardly stand it. The second man was a tax collector, a breaker of the law, an infidel who was spiritually unclean. He was a social leper and a religious outcast. He was such a sinner that he could hardly stand it.

Each morning and evening an atonement sacrifice was offered at the temple. Individuals offering personal prayers stood in the presence of the burning sacrifice. Jews believed that the best time to address God with personal requests was during the atonement sacrifice. Jewish prayer involved praise to God and petitions for the worshiper's needs.

Prayer at its best provides humble openness before God which leads to healing, not cover-ups. The Pharisee did neither. Instead, he boasted of his achievements and criticized the man next to him, while bragging to God about how he exceeded the demands of the law. (Bailey 145-146)

The Pharisee proceeded to list the deeds of his righteousness. Jews were expected to fast once a year on the day of atonement, but this man went far beyond the minimum, by fasting twice each week. Regarding the tithe, Jewish law required ten percent of one's grain, wine, and oil to be given to God. But this man tithed on everything he owned. His dedication to the Law puts most of us to shame. You wonder why he went beyond what the law expected of him?

Although other parables of Jesus might have been addressed to Pharisees, this is the only one that has a Pharisee as one of its main characters. The Pharisees, which means the "separated ones," formed a movement within Judaism committed to observing ritual purity and devotional piety toward God. They were held in high regard by the Jews, but also criticized by them for their self-righteousness and pride.

It is worth noting that when Jesus told the parable, he gave us the impression that he agreed with the Pharisee's claim that he was light years ahead of the tax collector in terms of his moral and religious righteousness. The Pharisee was an observer of the law; he was so good that it was not good for him. Maybe this was his downfall. He was

138

proud of his sacrifices and practices, which made it hard for him to be humble toward God. The Pharisee came to God with his hands full of pride.

It must have been uncomfortable for the Pharisee to see the tax collector next to him. It was customary for the unclean to stand at the eastern gate, a distance from where a righteous Pharisee would be. He could hardly look at this broken human being who symbolized everything he was bragging to God that he was not. We will always be able to find somebody less righteous than we are. If we must compare ourselves to anybody, let us compare ourselves to Jesus.

The tax collector's job was to collect market duties, tolls, and all kinds of taxes (income, property, sales and inheritance), and these collectors usually made a profit by over-charging people. They were neither liked nor respected by the Jews. The hearers of this parable would never have heard of a tax collector going to the temple to pray.

In contrast to the Pharisee, the tax collector entered the temple humble in spirit and genuine in repentance. Instead of lifting his head and hands in the customary posture of prayer, he addressed God without even looking up. His hands were clenched and struck his chest in a gesture of remorse and repentance. He brought nothing to God but a penitent heart. He cried in repentance and hope, "O God! Let this atonement be for my sins. Please forgive my sins." His hands were empty except for an honest confession of sin. He simply threw himself on the mercy of God. God was his only hope.

The tax collector went home justified before God and forgiven. That does not mean that he left home as an evil man and came back as a good man. It means that he left the encounter with God having received the forgiveness he humbly came for. Jesus exhorts us to come before God with the attitude of the tax collector and with awareness of our own sins and needs. When we honestly look at ourselves, we find the need to throw ourselves into the compassionate arms of God.

This parable warns us against the sin of pride. We learn from the Pharisee that all our good works lose their goodness without genuine humility. Jesus also tells us that having a religious spirit or doing the right religious things does not secure righteousness. Righteousness is a gift of God granted to those who come in humility and honestly request forgiveness and atonement for their sins.

Many of us think being a "good Christian" means being a victoriously cheerful and disciplined person who lives in careful accordance with biblical standards. There is an image we hold of how a "real Christian" should be and unfortunately it can lead us into an unhealthy trap. The trap is acting like a good Christian. We have an image to maintain so that other believers and God will accept us because of it, and this makes us feel good about ourselves. We cover up our problems and justify ourselves. We fall into the illusion of self-justification because of our need to be accepted by others. That need is driven by our own need for self-worth, and the fear of not being accepted and not belonging to the group.

Playing the pretending game with God does not work either. There can be no cover-ups, because our hearts are open to God's eyes. When we try to prove that we are good or better than others, God is not impressed. We all stand on the same level at the foot of the cross. We cannot save ourselves by our own efforts. We are accepted by God through grace. As the Apostle Paul puts it, "... it is by grace you have been saved, through faith—and this not from yourselves, it is the gift of God—not by works, so that no one can boast." (Ephesians 2:8-9)

I have met this Pharisee in other people and sometimes found him in me. He is unbearable. He's difficult to get along with because he's always right. He is a moral person whose morality has gone sour. Morality goes sour when it separates us from people who are different from us. God reaches out in love and forgiveness to each person who seeks grace with a humble spirit.

Humility is not highly valued in our society. Pride is valued and not just healthy pride. We are taught to put on a good act and to sell ourselves. Humility is often equated with low self-esteem or being a victim. However, true humility is not thinking less of ourselves, but thinking less about ourselves—being so free from thoughts about ourselves that we're free to focus our attention on God and on others.

Lynn learned this lesson in a new way while traveling in India one early morning in 1995. She writes of this experience: The noise and smog came filtering in with the early morning light through the chapel windows of the Mother House in Calcutta, India. I was leading a mission team and had the opportunity to spend a few minutes with Mother Teresa. After talking together for awhile, I asked

Mother Teresa how we could pray for her. Her response was not what I expected. She simply said, 'Pray that I might be humble.'

I have asked this same question to countless numbers of people over the years but have never received this prayer answer before. I realized I too had never asked God for humility. It has since become a regular prayer request of mine as well.

Mother Teresa's humility is clothed in strength and an awesome sense of holiness. It is not a humility that thinks less of herself but, rather, less about herself. This kind of humility frees us to be wholly focused on God and others knowing that, apart from God, we cannot fulfill our purpose.

The Midnight Visitor: *Living Prayerfully*

Luke 11:2-13

When you pray, say: "Father, Hallowed be your name, Your kingdom come. Give us each day our daily bread. Forgive us our sins, for we also forgive everyone who sins against us. And lead us not into temptation."

Then he said to them, "Suppose one of you has a friend, and he goes to him at midnight and says, 'Friend, lend me three loaves of bread, because a journeying friend has arrived at my house and I have nothing to set before him.' Then the one inside answers, 'Don't bother me. The door is already locked, and my children are with me in bed. I can't get up and give you anything.'

I tell you, though he will not get up and

give him the bread because he is his friend, yet because of the man's boldness (avoidance of shame) he will get up and give him as much as he needs."

"So I say to you: Ask and it will be given to you; seek and you will find; knock and the door will be opened to you. For everyone who asks receives; he who seeks finds; and to him who knocks, the door will be opened. Which of you fathers, if your son asks for a fish, will give him a snake instead? Or if he asks for an egg, will give him a scorpion? If you then, though you are evil, know how to give good gifts to your children, how much more will your Father in heaven give the Holy Spirit to those who ask him?"

The disciples had been with Jesus for quite a while—watching how he lived, listening to his teachings, observing his miracles and setting out to do ministry themselves. Their love for Jesus and their trust in him were growing. But one aspect of Jesus' life especially caught their interest —his prayer life. Jesus often went off into solitary places to pray—sometimes spending whole nights in prayer—but Jesus also prayed with the disciples. One day they decided to come out and ask him directly to teach them how to pray. It was not an unusual request for a disciple to make of his Rabbi. In response, Jesus taught them the Lord's Prayer as a model prayer and then told them this parable.

To understand what Jesus communicates to us today through this parable, we need to hear this prayer and story through the ears of Middle Eastern peasants of that day. Their first jolt came when Jesus addressed God as "abba," an Aramaic word for father that also expresses an intimate relationship. No one called God "Father," let alone "Dad" or "Daddy." It simply was not done. The name of God was too holy to be uttered, and absolute reverence was to be maintained at all times. But Jesus portrayed God as a loving and accessible parent who wants a close relationship with us. It was a startling concept. God is approachable, loving, and desires an intimate relationship with each of us.

That set the scene for the parable which followed. It began with the question, "Can you imagine going to a neighbor asking for bread to host a guest and the neighbor giving you an excuse about a locked door and sleeping children?" To many of us today the response would have been, "Sure I can!" But the disciples' response would have been, "No way. We cannot imagine that kind of response. It would be shameful!" The key to understanding Jesus' parable is to understand the Middle Eastern sense of responsibility toward guests and hospitality.

Guests in a Middle Eastern village are not only guests of the host, but also the guests of the entire community. Life could be rough for travelers, and survival depended on a strict code of hospitality. Furthermore, a Middle Eastern host would traditionally tell guests that the village or the community is honored by their visit. And thus, the host in the story requested his sleepy neighbor's help in uplifting the honor of the village by serving the guest a fresh loaf of bread. You see, if the guest was not properly welcomed and fed, it would bring shame to the whole community.

Now you may be asking yourself, if that is so, why bread and not a full-course meal? Bread is the most crucial part of the Middle Eastern diet. Everything is eaten with bread. Meals are eaten by using bread the same way that a spoon or fork is used in the west. The guest is always given a thin, flat loaf of bread nearly two feet across or a raised round loaf larger than the pita variety. Bread is the staple food of Middle Eastern life.

Jesus tells us that this man responded to his neighbor's request not because of the neighbor's persistence,—but because it was the right and responsible thing to do. Actually, the word "persistence or boldness" is mistranslated. The original ancient Greek word translates as "avoidance of shame." From reading the parable there is no evidence of persistence from the host. He simply called out to his neighbor and requested bread for the guest.

"What does shame have to do with it?" you may ask. Everything in Middle Eastern culture is controlled by the concept of shame and honor. Shame is to be avoided at all costs. A "sense of shame or shamelessness" helps us to avoid shameful actions. Hence, if the sleeping neighbor did not respond generously to the host's request, the neighbor's misconduct would be known by the entire community by morning, bringing shame upon the neighbor's family. Because of the desire to be honorable and avoid shame, the neighbor rose to the occasion and fulfilled the request of the host.

Jesus is, therefore, saying to his listeners, "If

you go to your neighbor with a request, even if it is midnight and very inconvenient, the neighbor will—out of desire to avoid shame, and to be honorable—respond to your genuine need."

Then Jesus strengthens his point by shifting from what is expected and done by a friend and neighbor to what is expected and done by a loving God. Our divine "Abba", our provider and sustainer to whom we go for our daily needs, is also a God of honor. Instead of a mere neighbor who acts out of avoidance of shame, God is a loving parent who is generous and eager to provide. Our requests are never a bother because, like a good parent, God cares for us much more than a neighbor can ever love us. We can therefore always and anytime call upon our divine "Abba" for our needs. If we can expect this neighbor to meet the host's needs, even at the most inconvenient times, how much more can we depend on a loving God who never sleeps?

Some of us reading this parable may not relate to the concept of a loving father or mother. This may be true if someone has grown up in a household with one or both parents who were absentees, abusive, distant, or anything but the kind of loving parent to whom Jesus refers. How can someone trust a parental figure if, in fact, they received a snake or a scorpion when they asked for a fish or an egg?

I believe that God's heart breaks with compassion for each one of us who suffer in this world. This was not God's plan for us. This brokenness in our midst is due to our separation from God and to the presence of evil in this world. Jesus offers a new reality to us—the opportunity to be adopted into God's family and experience the love, nurture and acceptance that the creator, the perfect parent, intended for us.

None of us were nurtured by perfect parents. Natural parents cannot meet all their children's needs. Parents try to do their best out of their own brokenness. Jesus encourages us always to forgive, because sometimes parents "know not what they do" too. In contrast, our divine "Abba" will neither leave us nor forsake us. God will heal us, not hurt us; God will give us new identities, a new beginning, and always unconditional love and acceptance. Jesus concludes that God will also give us the Holy Spirit to help us forgive, heal, be transformed, and live fruitful lives.

This parable struck home one October morning in 1989 while I was living in southern California. A heavy drizzle and thick blanket of darkness enshrouded my car as I left home with my family at 5 a.m. It filled me with a sense of discomfort despite my excitement about the trip ahead. We certainly needed this first rain of the fall season, but why today when I had such a long trip ahead? I had been invited to speak at a missions conference near San Francisco where I would represent the mission organization I directed, "Servants Among the Poor."

The '67 Ford Wagon chugged down the street, jam-packed with materials for the conference, luggage for several nights away, and added necessities like a large car jack, since our vehicle was old and suffered from many problems. My parents were with me anticipating a visit to family members they had not seen for 20 years, and my two-year-old daughter, Rebecca, lay asleep in my mother's arms.

Not even five minutes from the house my foreboding escalated into a nightmare. While turning at a stoplight the car skid and then hit a telephone pole head-on. Stunned, I tried to assess what happened. I had a sharp pain in my chest. My dad, in the passenger seat, had hit the windshield and his head was speared with glass. My mom was on the floor in the back screaming — and praying. Rebecca was also on the floor crying underneath my mom. Lynn quickly unfastened her seatbelt, which was piercing her abdomen. It was then that she realized she could not move.

The nightmare began taking increasingly alarming turns. I stood holding my daughter in the emergency room, my chest throbbing in pain from two cracked ribs. Rebecca was traumatized and her foot hurt, so she fussed and squirmed, yet insisted on being held. The nurse informed me I could not continue to go from bed to bed checking on Lynn, my dad and my mom. Exams and tests were being done. Things did not look good for my dad nor for Lynn, to say the least. In time, I was warned of the possibility that they might not make it through the night.

To make matters worse, our health insurance coverage would not begin for another ten days, since I had started a new job a few weeks before. Lynn had a ruptured colon, fractured spine, and broken orbital bone of her right eye. If she lived, she might not walk again. My dad suffered a heart attack from the stress of his concussion and multiple fractures of both legs. If they pulled through, they faced weeks of hospitalizations, multiple surgeries, and a long convalescence. The bill would run to over $100,000. Lynn's and my combined missionary salary was $14,000 per year.

I sat and waited, hour upon hour, helpless, my life out of control. At one point, I reached for my pocket Bible, and it fell open to a passage I had just taught on at the Union Rescue Mission of Los Angeles just the evening before—Hebrews 4:14-16:
"Therefore, since we have a great high priest who has gone through the heavens, Jesus the Son of God, let us hold firmly to the faith we profess. For we do not have a high priest who is unable to sympathize with our weaknesses, but we have one who has been tempted in every way, just as we are—yet was without sin. Let us then approach the throne of grace with confidence, so that we may receive mercy and find grace to help us in our time of need."

I quietly prayed in the emergency room. In the middle of the fear, trauma, and pain, I felt that God would carry us through this ordeal. I received peace, joy, and comfort. My divine "Abba" had heard my prayer.

God was gracious to my dad and to Lynn as they went through three weeks of hospitalization and several surgeries without complications. Lynn came within a fraction of a centimeter of becoming a paraplegic. We learned that people all across America had heard of the accident and were praying for us. Many came to visit and brought us help in many ways. Recovery at home for Lynn was progressing weeks ahead of schedule. The nightmare was turning around, but there was still the steady stream of hospital bills in the mail and calls from creditors demanding payment. I gave what I had and paid what I could weekly from my salary, but the balance was so far out of reach that a miracle was needed.

Then one day, months later, a bill arrived in the mail, which I read in disbelief. I read it a second time. The balance read, "Zero!" A mistake must have been made. Could this be true? Baffled as to what had happened, I called the hospital. They reassured me the balance had been paid in full!

Lynn's friend Wendie soon cleared up the mystery. Wendie worked for the HMO insurance company that picked up our account on the tenth day after the accident. She had spoken to her boss about us, telling him we were missionaries giving our lives to care for the poor and homeless at home and abroad. Wasn't there something the company could do? Her boss held a meeting and they did something unheard of for their company or any HMO. They paid the entire bill, including the ten days when we were not yet covered. God heard our prayers for help and provided every dollar needed!

We do not need to approach God with anxious hearts or persistence and manipulation. If we can expect the neighbor in this parable to meet the host's needs, even at the most inconvenient times, how much more can we depend on a loving God who never sleeps?

We can trust our heavenly Provider for all our needs. Our heavenly "Abba" wants the best for us. We can approach God with assurance and know that our prayers will be heard and that God's response will come at the right time. We don't need to feel ashamed to ask. Our legitimate needs will be met according to God's generous and loving will.

Parables to Live By

Part Three

The Father's Heart

The Prodigal Son:
Living Under Grace

Luke 15:1-24

Now the tax collectors and "sinners" were all gathering around to hear Jesus. But the Pharisees and the teachers of the law muttered, "This man welcomes sinners and eats with them."

Then Jesus told them this parable: "Suppose one of you has a hundred sheep and loses one of them. Does he not leave the ninety-nine in the open country and go after the lost sheep until he finds it? And when he finds it, he joyfully puts it on your shoulders and goes home. Then he calls his friends and neighbors together and says 'Rejoice with me; I have found my lost sheep.' I tell you that in the same way there will be more rejoicing in heaven over one sinner who repents than over ninety-nine righteous persons who do not need to repent.

"Or suppose a woman has ten silver coins and loses one. Does she not light a lamp, sweep the house and search carefully until she finds it? And when she finds it, she calls her friends and neighbors together and says, 'Rejoice with me; I have found my lost coin.' In the same way, I tell you, there is rejoicing in the presence of the angels of God over one sinner who repents."

Then Jesus told them this parable: "There was a man who had two sons. The younger one said to his father, 'Father, give me my share of the estate.' So he divided his property between them. Not long after that, the younger son got together all he had, set off for a distant country and there squandered his wealth in wild living. After he had spent everything, there was a severe famine in that whole country, and he began to be in need. So he went and hired himself out to a citizen of that country, who sent him to his fields to feed pigs. He longed to fill his stomach with the pods that the pigs were eating, but no one gave him anything.

"When he came to his senses, he said, 'How many of my father's hired men have food to spare, and here I am starving to death! I will set out and go back to my father and say to him: "Father, I have sinned against heaven and against you. I am no longer worthy to be called your son; make me like one of your hired men." So he got up and went to his father.

"But while he was still a long way off, his father saw him and was filled with compassion for him; he ran to his son; threw his arms around him and kissed him.

"The son said to him, 'Father, I have sinned against heaven and against you. I am no longer worthy to be called your son.'

"But the father said to his servants, 'Quick! Bring the best robe and put it on him. Put a ring on his finger and sandals on his feet. Bring the fattened calf and kill it. Let's have a feast and celebrate. For this son of mine was dead and is alive again; he was lost and is found.' So they began to celebrate."

H ave you ever wondered, if Jesus came back to earth whether some churches would feel uncomfortable having him around their congregations? You see, the Pharisees and the scribes in Jesus' time—the religious leaders of the day—felt the same about Jesus. And they had some moral reasons for the way they felt. Jesus hung around the wrong crowd.

There is a saying in the Middle East: "Tell me who your friends are and I will tell you who you are."

Jesus befriended tax collectors, shepherds, the poor, prostitutes, and people with leprosy. Today's equivalent may be gang members, loan sharks, alcoholics, homeless, hustlers, hookers, and people with AIDS. The people who consider themselves righteous and moral frequently look down on those types of people. Jesus spent his time with them. I ask myself: if I had only three years to accomplish Jesus' great mission, would I spend my time with this crowd?

In the third century C.E., the pagan Celsus and the Christian Origen engaged in a debate on Christianity. In the course of the debate Celsus reportedly declared, "When most teachers go forth to teach, they cry, 'Come to me, you who are clean and worthy,' and they are followed by the highest caliber of people available, but your silly master (Jesus) cries, 'Come to me, you who are down and beaten by life,' and so he accumulates around him the rag, tag and bobtail of humanity."

Origen's response to Celsus' attack was profound and filled with the wisdom of God: "Yes," he said, "they are the rag, tag and bobtail of humanity. But Jesus does not leave them that way. Out of material you would have thrown away as useless, he fashions people, giving them back their self-respect, enabling them to stand on their feet and look God in the eyes. They were cowed, cringing, broken things. But the Son has set them free." Transformation is what Jesus brings to broken lives.

Jesus was invited into the homes of the rag, tag and bobtail of humanity. He ate and drank with them. The religious leaders of the time considered this a scandal. In Matthew 11:18, Jesus tells us that he was called a glutton and a drunkard by the religious leaders, and in Luke 15 the Pharisees were complaining that he welcomed sinners and ate with them. In response to this criticism, Jesus gave three parables. The first parable was about the lost sheep and the shepherd who left his flock to go after the one lost sheep.

The second was about the lost coin and the woman who did everything possible to find it, and rejoiced greatly when she did. These first two parables were a preparation for the third—a masterpiece. The early church leaders called it the Gospel within the Gospel. Charles Dickens said that the parable of the Prodigal Son was the finest short story ever written.

It is a simple story. It could have happened anywhere at anytime—even now, in our very homes. Teenagers all over America get frustrated and disillusioned with life at home. They believe life has to be better elsewhere, so they run away in alarming numbers. But it isn't only young people; it is estimated that hundreds of thousands of American adults "run away" every year. The average adult male runaway is usually a successful business executive or professional, age 44 to 50, college-educated. The pressure finally pushes him to the edge. Some turn to alcohol and drugs; some have nervous breakdowns. Many simply drop out or disappear. Sometimes families track them down, and usually they're found in nearby cities living in low-rent sections of town, working at manual-labor jobs and seeking anonymity and irresponsibility.

Just as many women run away as men, except women who do so are usually younger—around 35 to 40. They marry early, have children, stay at home, and feel unappreciated and trapped. Searching for a better and more satisfying life, one day they escape.

In this story Jesus tells us of a father who had two sons. One was a playboy and the other a farm boy. The younger one, the playboy, said to his father, "Give me my share of your estate." Within the Middle

East culture, that son would really be saying, "I do not want to stay in your household any longer. I can't wait for you to die so that I can start living." The younger son is sick of home.

There is no custom in the Middle East that supports this son's request. In fact, it was highly discouraged in rabbinical teachings of the day. A well-respected rabbi contemporary to Jesus' time said that there were three cries that God would not answer: "He who has money and lends it without a witness; he who acquires a master; and he who transfers his property to his children in his lifetime." (Bailey 164)

The story continues. The father divided his property between his two sons. According to tradition, the younger got a third and the older got two thirds.

The father knows that sons have the basic need to choose on their own, even if they make wrong choices in the process of becoming mature adults. This father knew that it is human to make mistakes, and learn from these mistakes.

The younger son sold his share, gathered everything he owned and traveled to a distant land. I expect that it was a quick sell, possibly 70¢ on the dollar. He could very well have sold it to a Gentile, as his community would most likely have had a hard time taking advantage of the deal. If he did this, the younger son would be inviting someone the Jews considered unclean into the community, thus cutting himself off socially from the family and the community where he grew up.

Assuming this was a very real possibility, by Jewish tradition of the time a ceremony would then be performed by the family in which the community took part. It was called the "qesasah" or "cutting off" ceremony. A member of the family—most likely the older son—would bring a barrel full of parched corn and nuts to the center of town, followed by the kids from the community. The barrel would be dropped and broken while announcing that the younger son was cut off from the community. The kids would take the nuts and corn and run throughout the town, declaring the news. This son was now officially cut off from the community and publicly humiliated.

And then—I wonder what the people would have said about the father. Maybe they said "This old fool did not know how to discipline and raise his son. Maybe he's not qualified anymore for public leadership. Certainly his house is not in order. He should not serve as an elder in the community." It is always easy to judge when we don't have all the information and when we don't know the full story.

The story continues and Jesus tells us that the son spent all the money on wild living. You name it—drinking, prostitution, gambling—the kid probably did it. Then a famine struck the land where the younger son was living. He ran out of money, grew hungry, and was so in need, he hired himself out to a citizen of that country who sent him to care for his pigs. Can you imagine a Jewish man caring for pigs?

Jesus' listeners at this point must have been repulsed. No respectful Jew would have ever taken such a job, for pigs were considered unclean; pork is not kosher. But this young man was at rock bottom. He even wanted to eat the pigs' food! He was hungry, but people valued the pigs more than the man who cared for them. This is very true in a time of famine. Animals and things generally are valued more than people. In addition, now the younger son could not observe the Sabbath or even come to God in prayer, because he was ceremonially unclean, being in constant contact with pigs. He was without hope and God in this dark world.

The son knew he had broken his relationship with his father, his family, his community, and with God. He was now in despair.

He was hungry, lonely, homeless, lost and confused.

We are all created with a strong desire to belong to God and others, and he started to feel a deep need inside. He was aware that his life was out of control, and that realization required courage. He looked at the quality of his current relationships and all he saw were pigs. The quality of our relationships is the barometer of our emotional and spiritual health. If we look at our relationship with God and that of our family and friends, we will be able to see how healthy we are emotionally and spiritually. The young man's eyes were opened, and he did not like what he saw.

This story touches us because it tells how lost we can get when we run away from God and responsibility. We find ourselves in a jam whenever we try to run away. We should pray that in the midst of our desire to run away from whatever we face, we will discover a God who loves us and who gives us a sense of belonging and peace.

The prodigal son realized how foolish he had been to run away from home. Now there are two responses that can take place when we look deep inside of ourselves. One is to see what is wrong—what mistakes were made. The feelings of guilt may cause us to repent and ask for forgiveness from the people we have hurt and from God. We can learn from our mistakes.

The second response is a damaging one. We look deep inside of ourselves and we see despair, ugliness, and shame; we feel that we not only made mistakes—we are a mistake. The feelings which should cause guilt instead turn to toxic shame. Consequently, we do not seek restoration, but rather self-destruction.

The blessing of this story is that this son knew that he had made mistakes. The first step out of the pigpen is to recognize who we are and what we have done to get into the mess.

The second step is to repent and ask forgiveness for our mistakes from God and the people we have harmed. Returning to God is what repentance is all about. Repentance is a complete reorientation of our lives. The prodigal son realized that he was going in the wrong direction in his life, so he turned around and headed toward home. Instead of running away from God and people, we turn around and run toward God and others to receive love and care from them. Instead of running from our problems and responsibilities, we turn around to face them with God's help.

One reason I believe the son was able to make this decision is that he knew what kind of father was waiting for him at home— a father with amazing love and grace. He relied on the love of his father. If you remember, the father did not shame the son, even when he made the wrong decision. He extended his love to him; he left the door open for his return.

President Lincoln was once asked how he would treat the rebellious Southerners if they were defeated and were willing to return to the Union of the United States. Lincoln responded, "I will treat them as if they had never been away." Jesus says that we are loved even after we have rebelled and run away from God. If we return, God will treat us as though we had never been away.

The son understood that reconciliation would require effort and change on his part, too. He was willing to be a hired servant in his father's house, working to earn his living. We can tell he had a repentant heart—there was no self-justification and no demands that he put on anyone. He probably couldn't make full restitution, but he would do what he could. He put his trust in God and he took a trip back home in faith.

The father heard that his son was coming, and he went running joyfully to meet him with a heart full of compassion. He put his arms around him and kissed him. In the Middle East, an old man does not run. He walks with dignity. To run, he had to hold his robes up and show his bare legs. The father decided to look like a fool, so his son did not have to go through humiliation in front of the community. He would take the son's shame on himself. He was saying, "I love my son, and I have forgiven him. If you have anything to say to him, you say it to me."

The son's speech is word-for-word what he had practiced on his way home, but he was on his feet and in his father's arms, not kneeling. As soon as the son says that he is no longer worthy to be called a son, the father has heard more than enough. The father's response is to treat him not only as a beloved son, but as an honored guest! Kissing his son was a sign of reconciliation and acceptance. Then he called for a robe. The son's emaciated body was probably smelly and quite dirty. His father covered him with a robe like the clean robe of righteousness (Zechariah 3:3-4). Next he put a ring on his finger—a signet ring signifying the granting of authority to the son. Placing "shoes on his feet" implies not only that the son came home barefoot, but implies that he was now a master, not a servant. Then the celebration started. The father called for a fattened calf to be killed. He intended for the whole community to celebrate with him. His beloved son was home again!

This is forgiveness. Deep in our soul, we all have a need to feel that we are accepted, respected, understood, forgiven, trusted, and loved for who we are. All the rebellion and confusion that we go through in life makes us aware of our need for connecting with and belonging to someone we can truly trust. But we will be disappointed if we expect that people alone will meet all our needs. People cannot meet them; only God can.

God sent Jesus to lead us out of despair. God holds our hands all the way home. How easy it is to find ourselves drifting away from home, but we find God giving love and abundant grace in tangible ways during our most desperate moments. God finds us again and again and brings us back home.

For over ten years, I have known Jeffrey, a sweet, sensitive, bright young man, but also very troubled. In fact, shortly after first meeting him, I received several phone calls from people who knew him, warning me to be careful and not to get too close. Jeffrey only caused problems everywhere he went, they said. Psychological reports from his doctors documented his several attempts at suicide. One doctor predicted he'd be dead by the age of 26; Jeffrey was 25 years old at that time. But the Jeffrey I grew to know was someone who was in a great deal of pain, haunted by memories from his childhood abuse, sexually and emotionally, and by many destructive decisions he had made through the years.

Jeffrey's physical and sexual abuse began at

age seven at the hands of his stepfather, an alcoholic minister. Not only was he constantly abused at home, but as a preteen, Jeffrey was also drawn into a homosexual relationship with his teacher. Just after his 13th birthday, Jeffrey fled to Hollywood to become a movie star. He lived on the streets of Hollywood and Los Angeles surviving any way he could. He ate out of garbage cans, prostituted his body, and did whatever was necessary to survive.

After five years on the streets he sought a shelter which reached out to runaway youth. With its help he went back to school, received his diploma, and proceeded on to college courses. He even secured jobs from time to time, but his cycles of depression and ongoing inner pain often led him to miss work and eventually get fired. He gained over 100 pounds in a few short months. Five years and six suicide attempts later, he came to the mission not knowing what else to do—depressed and now diagnosed HIV-positive. His journey through treatment and counseling lasted for several years. During this time the pain and depression got almost unbearable.

Jeffrey's story is too long and too painful to be fully told here. But when I look at Jeffrey and the many men and women like him who have lived on the streets or have been emotionally, physically, or sexually abused, I am in awe of the faith they often have. They are incredible people who believe in a God who gives life and who heals. Perhaps their faith is strong because they have been in some of the same circumstances as Jesus. Like him, they have been beaten and hated. Like him, they have been homeless. His journey home ended abruptly outside Jerusalem on a hill next to the garbage dump. He ended his life just as he began it—homeless. Jesus has no trouble loving the people of the streets. They have shared and suffered so many things in common.

Today Jeffrey is doing well and making it one day at a time. He is over 40 years old—

more than 11 years beyond the age when he was supposed to have died. Life is still not easy for him and is sometimes a day-to-day struggle. But Jeffrey has completed his bachelor's degree in Chemistry with a 4.0 average and is enrolled in a masters/Ph.D. program. After eight years of treatment for the AIDS virus, he is no longer HIV-positive. The doctors wonder if he was misdiagnosed all this time, but Jeffrey believes he's been healed. Jeffrey puts his love and hope in God, who was willing to bring another prodigal home.

The prodigal sons and daughters of our streets do not tend to come to rescue missions once and then stay. Many times they return to the streets, but they definitely leave a mark in our hearts. We try to remember joyful moments we shared together in God's spirit. We hold tight to these memories, waiting for their next return, and in some cases looking for them on the streets and reminding them that there is a caring family waiting for them at the mission. Some end up in jails, some die from a drug overdose, violence or physical causes, but others come home and settle in, finding comfort, belonging, and purpose in God's house.

The Elder Son:
Living Responsibly

Luke 15: 25-32

"Meanwhile, the older son was in the field. When he came near the house, he heard music and dancing. So he called one of the servants and asked him what was going on. 'Your brother has come,' he replied, 'and your father has killed the fattened calf because he has him back safe and sound.'

The older brother became angry and refused to go in. So his father went out and pleaded with him. But he answered his father, 'Look! All these years I've been slaving for you and never disobeyed your orders. Yet you never gave me even a young goat so I could celebrate with my friends. But when this son of yours who has squandered your property with

189

prostitutes comes home, you kill the fat-
tened calf for him!'
"'My son,' the father said, 'you are al-
ways with me, and everything I have is
yours. But we had to celebrate and be
glad, because this brother of yours was
dead and is alive again; he was lost and
is found.' "

T he story could very well have ended
beautifully with a celebration, reconciliation, and new life. But Jesus, the
master storyteller, does not end his message
there. You remember that Jesus' audience
was comprised of sinners and Pharisees.
There was one more important message
Jesus wanted them to know.

And so the story continues. The older
brother comes back from a long day working
in the field. Most of us are very proud of
young, hard-working men and women who
end up as civic leaders and elders in our

communities. People like them are the mortar that holds society together. Without them, very little can be accomplished.

Although the dominant mood on the farm that night was one of joy, there were at least two who were unhappy: the fattened calf and the older son. The older son heard the sound of music, festivity, and laughter coming from his father's house. At first he was probably confused, then furious, and refused to set foot in his father's house. He despised his father's joy. What was his father happy about?

He thought to himself, "The loser came back, bringing shame and humiliation to us. What will my friends say?" He rejected his father's grace toward his younger brother. He would not share in the celebration. He wanted his younger brother thrown out of the house; he wanted him to pay for his mistakes and for shaming the family. He didn't want to be seen associating with him. "After all, the playboy got his part of the estate—all the rest is lawfully mine. I earned it! This kid knew what was coming to him. What is he back for? Everything that is left in this house is mine; all the robes, rings, every pair of sandals, every fattened calf, and, especially, all the recognition and the love in this house is mine."

I wonder who was now far from the father's heart! The older brother was as far away from his father's heart as the younger brother was in the faraway country. It is possible to be lost in a foreign country, but it is also possible to be lost living right at home in one's father's house. It is but a matter of the heart.

Then the good father went out for the second time to bring in a son. This time, his older son insulted him in front of the guests by refusing to celebrate what was so dear to a father's heart. Jesus draws another beautiful picture of the grace of God. The older son symbolizes the religious person—the one who knows right from wrong. He is the one who supposedly understood the father's heart and will. Here, the father for the second time on the same day accepts public humiliation, as the community notices the older son's absence and his refusal to attend his father's celebration.

The father urged his son to come in and celebrate the return of his brother. You can hear the compassion in the father's heart for his older son. He repeats the promise to him, "Son, all that I have is yours; nothing is being withheld from you. Come into the feast." We can feel the father's gentle, patient, forgiving love for both sons. Neither is rejected.

Now the older brother has become lost, alone and outside the father's house, yet so close to the door. He didn't understand his father anymore; he may have even lost respect for him. In fact, his friends may have become more important to him than his father. You wonder why he stayed this long in the house? Maybe it was out of fear of losing his inheritance. You heard him say to the father, "All these years, I have served you." Like his brother, all he really wanted was the benefits, except that he was willing to work to get them.

If the older brother had really known the father's heart, he would have been there alongside his father, welcoming his younger brother, hugging him, kissing him, and inviting him back home. What else should an older brother do?

You recall the two parables prior to this one—the shepherd who left the 99 sheep to look for the one, or the woman who stopped all her work just to look for the lost coin? Here we have a man who loses his only brother, and what does he do? He goes back to work as if nothing happened and he does not even want to eat or drink with him when he returns. What should an older brother do? He should have gone to look for his lost brother in the foreign country. Jesus did exactly that.

You will recall that these three parables were introduced by Jesus in response to the criticism of the religious people of the day. They could not understand why Jesus associated with the unrighteous. Jesus is telling his religious listeners, "You are no different from the older brother. You do not want to eat and drink with the unrighteous or welcome them into the father's house. But I will!"

Jesus is the true first Son of God, the heir of God's house. He can say, "All of this is mine," and of Jesus, God can say, "this is my son, whom I love. With him I am well pleased." Jesus is the true heir of all, in heaven and on earth. But gladly he shares it with us.

Jesus gives it all. He made himself nothing, taking the very nature of a servant, as Paul tells us, and gave all to save his brothers and sisters (Philippians 2:6-8). If sinners wait upon their older brothers to rescue them, they will all die in the pigpen. But Jesus left his home with God, became poor, and searched for us. He found us tired, lost, hungry, and thirsty for God's love and intimacy. He put his arms around us and invited us to come on home.

Some think this sounds too easy or too simple. Is there neither judgment nor a price to pay for forgiveness? Yes, there was a great price paid for forgiveness. The great feast is not prepared by the killing of a fattened calf, but by the sacrificial killing of the Lamb of God. God does not believe in cheap forgiveness. A great price was paid and God had to listen to the cries of Jesus on the cross, watch Jesus die, and not lift a finger to help. Jesus proved that love with the last breath of his life and drop of his blood on the cross at Calvary.

Not too long before Mother Teresa died, Lynn had the opportunity to spend some quality time with her in Calcutta. When asked whether there was any message she would like the team to bring back to America for her, Mother Teresa took the hand of a team member next to her and began touching each finger saying:

> **I** was hungry and you gave me something to eat
> **I** was thirsty and you gave me something to drink
> **I** was naked and you clothed me
> **I** was a stranger and you invited me in
> **I** was sick and imprisoned and you visited me

Then on the next hand she continued:
> **I** want
> **I** will
> **B**y God's grace to
> **B**e
> **H**oly

Then pressing the two hands together in a gesture of prayer she concluded: "Unite these together in prayer. That is my message for America."

I believe that to live responsibly in God's

house, we are called to go and find the lost and broken of the world—to reach out and serve among the poor, the addicts, the prisoners, the lonely, the sick, the persecuted, and the rejected.

We are called to bring compassion through our actions, realizing that we are ministering to God's broken heart in an act of worship. This, coupled with our earnest desire for holiness, opens us to God's transforming spirit.

Sources and Selected Bibliography

Alexander, F. & Rollins, M. <u>Pass It On: The Story of Bill Wilson and How the A.A. Message Reached the World</u>. New York: Alcoholics Anonymous World Services, 1984, pp.121.

Bailey, Kenneth. <u>Poet and Peasant and Through Peasant Eyes</u>. Grand Rapids, MI: William B. Eerdmans, 1976.

Cox, James W., ed. <u>Best Sermons 3</u>. San Francisco: Harper, 1990, pp. 22-28.

Cox, James W., ed. <u>The Ministers Manual 1989</u>. San Francisco: Harper, 1988, pp. 174-176.

Cox, James W., ed. <u>Best Sermons 6</u>. San Francisco: Harper, 1993, pp. 261-267.

Cox, James W., ed. <u>The Ministers Manual 1987</u>. San Francisco: Harper, 1987, pp. 322-324.

Cox, James W., ed. <u>Best Sermons 7</u>. San Francisco: Harper, 1994, pp. 65-71.

Cox, James W., ed. <u>Best Sermons 5</u>. San Francisco: Harper, 1992, pp. 265-271.

Fee, Gordon D. & Stuart, Douglas. How To Read The Bible For All Its Worth. Grand Rapids, MI: Zondervan, 1982.

Heineman, William. Josephus, Jewish Antiquities. Cambridge: Harvard University Press, 1961.

Kutz, Ernest. Not-God: A History of Alcoholics Anonymous. Center City, MN: Hazelden, 1991, pp.125.

Linn, Dennis, Sheila and Matthew. Belonging: Bonds of Healing and Recovery. New York: Paulist Press, 1993, pp. 64.

About the Author

John G. Samaan was born and raised in Alexandria, Egypt. He began serving among the poor as a teenager by visiting families in the slums of Alexandria. For the past 40 years he has been involved in ministries that serve the poor, both in the United States and abroad.

He ministered in the heart of Skid Row, Los Angeles, for several years. For the last 15 years, John has served as President of the Boston Rescue Mission. John is also the founder of Stewardship Consulting Group. He holds a Bachelor of Science in Engineering, a Master of Business Administration, a Master of Divinity degree, and is a Certified Fund Raising Executive (CFRE).

John has earned recognition from President Clinton and Vice President Gore as well as leaders of the cities of Boston and Los Angeles for his service among the poor. Most recently, John received the Boston Celtics Hero Award during their World Championship 2007-2008 season.

Thank you for taking the time to read Parables to Live By *and for your continuous support of the Boston Rescue Mission.*

The cost to produce this book was minimal and no donations designated to serve our guests were used for this project. All proceeds from the sale of this book go to benefit poor and homeless men and women.

After you read this book, I'd love to hear from you. You can write or e-mail your thoughts, questions, or comments to us at:

jsamaan@bostonrescuemission.com

To order additional copies, please send your request and a donation of $5.00 per book to:

Boston Rescue Mission
P.O. Box 120069
Boston, MA 02112-0069
(617) 338-9000 ext. 1216
www.bostonrescuemission.com